"Can you rebuild marital trust after sexual sin? Yes, and Jason Martinkus and Stephen Arterburn will show you how. Jason and his wife, Shelley, take you on their deeply personal and spiritual journey from betrayal to trust. Read this book and apply the principles, and you, too, can regain trust in your marriage."

> —DR. DAVID CLARKE, Christian psychologist, speaker, and author
> of *I Don't Want a Divorce*

"This book opens the reader's eyes to the difficult truth and reality of what it takes to rebuild trust in a relationship devastated by sexual betrayal. My marriage would not have survived without God's grace and the wisdom and essential guidance found in *Worthy of Her Trust*. Any man committed to winning back his wife at all costs needs to read this book!"

> —CURTIS, Arizona

"No matter how tragic and seemingly irreparable your marriage may be, there is hope. My husband wanted to rebuild trust in a hopeless situation. He learned and continues to implement the amends matrix, and he has kept 242 days of the T-30 journal. We have not only experienced reconciliation, but we have been restored individually. For that I am eternally grateful! If you are both ready to let God redeem the past and help you build trust again, *Worthy of Her Trust* will show you how."

> —SUSAN, Colorado

"Finally, for one of the darkest periods of any relationship, Jason has delivered a no-nonsense, inspired approach for rebuilding shattered trust. By sharing his compassion and insight, he has opened the door for true transformation and growth. This is a must-read book if moving forward is your goal."

> —DAVE, California

*"Worthy of Her Trust* is the go-to, step-by-step resource for professionals or anyone seeking guidance through the trust-building process. Martinkus presents a model of relationship intimacy—based on closeness and honesty—a connection that becomes both the context and motivation for the redemptive journey."

—BOB SKLAR, LMFT

# WORTHY OF HER TRUST

# WORTHY

## WHAT YOU NEED TO DO TO REBUILD

# OF HER

## SEXUAL INTEGRITY AND WIN HER BACK

# TRUST

## STEPHEN ARTERBURN
### AND
## JASON B. MARTINKUS

### WATERBROOK
PRESS

Worthy of Her Trust
Published by WaterBrook Press
12265 Oracle Boulevard, Suite 200
Colorado Springs, Colorado 80921

Trade Paperback ISBN 978-1-60142-536-2
eBook ISBN 978-1-60142-537-9

Published in the United States by WaterBrook Multnomah, an imprint of the Crown Publishing Group, a division of Random House LLC, New York, a Penguin Random House Company.

WATERBROOK and its deer colophon are registered trademarks of Random House LLC.

Library of Congress Cataloging-in-Publication Data
Arterburn, Stephen, 1953–
   Worthy of her trust : what you need to do to rebuild sexual integrity and win her back / Stephen Arterburn and Jason B. Martinkus. — First Edition.
        pages cm
   ISBN 978-1-60142-536-2 (paperback) — ISBN 978-1-60142-537-9 (electronic) 1. Sex addicts—Religious life. 2. Sex addiction—Religious aspects—Christianity. 3. Christian men—Sexual behavior. 4. Marriage—Religious aspects—Christianity. 5. Christian men—Religious life. I. Martinkus, Jason B. II. Title.
   BV4596.S42A78 2014
   248.8'627—dc23

                                                                2014004504

Printed in the United States of America
2014—First Edition

10 9 8 7 6 5 4 3 2 1

SPECIAL SALES
Most WaterBrook Multnomah books are available at special quantity discounts when purchased in bulk by corporations, organizations, and special-interest groups. Custom imprinting or excerpting can also be done to fit special needs. For information, please e-mail SpecialMarkets@WaterBrookMultnomah.com or call 1-800-603-7051.

*From Jason: I dedicate this book to my wife, Shelley. Without your willingness to wait on God, we wouldn't have made it. Thank you for not leaving me. Without your wholehearted support, I couldn't have written this. Thank you for allowing our marriage to be the canvas on which God is painting a profound portrait. You continue to amaze me.*

———◇———

*From Stephen: I would also like to dedicate this book to Shelley. Her willingness to speak of her experience to the men who have gone through the Every Man's Battle Workshop has changed the hearts of many. Thanks for your bravery there and allowing us to share your story here.*

# CONTENTS

## PART 3: MENDING WOUNDS

## PART 4: TRUST-BUILDING TACTICS

# FOREWORD

## A Word to Husbands
## from Stephen Arterburn

I don't know of any assignment more difficult (but more worthwhile) than the job of regaining a wife's trust.

She trusted you enough to marry you, but the bond of trust has been broken. So many men just walk away when they have failed and broken the heart of a loving spouse. They think it's better to walk away and start over than do the work to heal a wound that is so deep. Many men think they will be better off, but they won't. They walk away and take their shame—and the knowledge that they walked away when they most needed to step up. In fact, research shows that those who walk away are not happier later than those who stay and work through the problem.

Using the National Survey of Families and Households, a team from the Institute for American Values (comprised of Linda J. Waite, Don Browning, William J. Doherty, Maggie Gallagher, Ye Luo, and Scott M. Stanley) developed a 2002 report titled *Does Divorce Make People Happy? Findings from a Study of Unhappy Marriages.* Couples surveyed in the late eighties who rated their marriages as unhappy were surveyed again five years later—after some had divorced, separated, or stayed married. The findings were very convincing but seemed to have little impact on the way the world viewed divorce as a solution for unhappiness. The world seems to remain unconvinced. Here are some of the conclusions reached from the study:

- Unhappily married adults who divorced or separated were no happier, on average, than unhappily married adults who stayed married.
- Divorce for unhappily married adults did not reduce their symptoms of depression, raise their self-esteem, or increase their

sense of mastery, on average, compared to unhappy spouses who
stayed married.

- Two out of three unhappily married adults who avoided divorce
  or separation ended up happily married five years later.

The obvious point here is that divorce does not fix things. But I have to
add that staying together without doing the needed work does not fix things
either. And without work, no trust will be regained.

If you have become dependent on a lifestyle that lacks sexual integrity
and now want to be free forever, you're embarking on a path that is highly
possible and being lived out by thousands of men. If you are married, your
wife is on a path also. The best thing you can do to help her heal is to build
a life of consistency, predictability, compassion, and connection to her heart.
She has been through a lot. Don't expect her to just simply "get over it."

I am so glad you obtained this book and are on a path to healing and
rebuilding trust in your marriage. You may not realize this, but in the process
you are also rebuilding the core of your manhood. You are constructing a
new man who is free of addiction and obsession. You are building a man you
can count on and be proud of when you look in the mirror. You are building
a man of integrity, consistency, and clarity—a man who can be counted on
and trusted.

You are that man or you can become that man, and this book will provide a path to help you be and remain the man God wants you to be.

In 1999 I was grateful to receive a phone call from Fred Stoeker with an
invitation to help him write *Every Man's Battle*. The book later became a
series, which to date has sold over three million copies. As the Every Man
series developed over many years and numerous projects, I saw, witnessed,
and heard from thousands of men and women who were on a path of sin and
destruction who are now healing, growing, and living a life of freedom. One
of the needs that became obvious from the books and the stories of these
struggles was the need to help men rebuild and regain trust from their broken

spouse. When Jason Martinkus developed the relevant and powerful information contained in this book, I was more than happy to help out. Both of us want to see you walk with a new sense of purpose and meaning as well as to break free from any shame that might drag you back into a relapse.

Over the years I have made a few discoveries that have helped me in my own journey toward wholeness and healing. One of those discoveries is the power of shame. Shame is the cancer that can completely eat away a soul. It is most likely what kept you from getting help long ago. You probably believed that the shame of being known and openly dealing with your problem was greater than the shame of leading a double life full of secrets and duplicity. Shame kept you in the problem for other reasons too. Every time that shame started to overwhelm you and drive you toward the worst of who you had become, you had an instant fix for the feeling. You acted out or "acted in," filling your mind with the forbidden. And every time you did, shame grew just a little bit more, took a little stronger hold, and continued to erode at your life and your connections with others.

I think shame is one of the more powerful triggers to bring a man back into lust and unfaithfulness. It makes us feel unworthy of God's love or the love of a spouse. So in our secrecy, isolation, and pain, when we feel like we don't deserve the taste of transformation we have experienced, we jump right back into the cycle that created all of the shame in the first place.

Once I was counseling a minister who had fallen from the pinnacle of ministry success. There was no one more respected in his community; no church was bigger or growing faster; no man felt more pain as a result of God's amazing gifts to him bearing such amazing fruit. When he came to me, he had been out of ministry for some time and he really wanted to change. I could have given him a *Life Recovery Bible* or a textbook on addiction. But instead I suggested we study shame. I wanted him to understand everything he could about shame so he would grasp the condition that had kept him down, as well as the enemy that would drive him to relapse. And he did. I believe his recovery has been strong because of his willingness to follow a restoration plan coupled with his great knowledge of shame.

If you are struck by a club, a rock, or a fist, it lands on the outside of you. The damage is painful but will heal. But shame is something that hits your soul from the inside. It doesn't heal. It scars and rips you up from the inside out. It becomes you, and you become it. You feel shameful, and so you predictably do shameful things. And while you are engulfed by shame, life feels so hopeless, because there is no place to take it and deal with it, and because the added shame of being known would be too great to handle.

When I paid to abort a pregnancy that was a result of my own addiction, I woke up with an overwhelming sense of shame for what I had done. A man's role in reproduction ends at conception, and then it is his duty to provide for and protect the life he has created. But I did not do that. I woke up realizing I had moved to destroy my own child because I was too much of a coward to do the right and responsible thing—providing for my baby and being there for her and her mother. My internal shame injured my health, and I ended up with about seventy ulcers that would kill me if something did not change. I lived as if the worse I made myself feel, the more deserving I would be of God's forgiveness. Of course I could never do enough, and my shame distorted the man I was and cut me off from others. And it cured nothing. I could not feel enough shame to stop the addiction. So, sadly, I went back to my promiscuous ways after the abortion.

To turn it all around, I had to surrender my pride and shame as well as my efforts to fix myself or earn favor from God. I sought help and began to open up to my parents, a minister, a counselor, friends, and my boss. And as I brought my shame into the open, its power began to erode.

I hope you have discovered that the sickness of your secrets and the power they have over your life diminish greatly when you simply open up rather than stew secretly in your shame.

The reason this is so important is that a shame-filled person is not a trustworthy person. When shame is the definer of your life, integrity won't be. That powerful shame will grab you when you least expect it and drag you down even further.

I challenge you to look at the shame you still possess within you. Open up about it and do whatever you can to resolve it. God does not want shame in your life. It separates you from God and from those you love. And life is so much easier when you don't have to work to compensate for it.

You have made a decision to change your life. You are making an impact on the world simply by showing that transformation is possible. People around you have seen that what you once valued most is now meaningless to you. I honor you for these bold moves. But the toughest move you may face is regaining the trust of your spouse. It takes more time than most people want to give it. It takes an ironclad commitment to consistency, predictability, and accountability. But every time you are where you say you will be and do what you say you will do, you build security in her heart that will enable her to trust you again.

I am praying God's blessing upon you and your wife. I want her to trust you and respond to your dedication to winning her back and becoming the man you need to be.

If you have any comments or questions, I would love to hear from you at sarterburn@newlife.com.

God bless you each day of your journey.

# "How Can I Ever Trust You Again?"

There is no response sufficient to answer the question posed above, no response that quite matches the gravity of a question originating from a place so deep within that it seems almost unanswerable.

What elements might the answer contain? Time? Space? Specific tasks? Counseling? Prayer? Words? Actions? Only God?

The answer can feel beyond reach. And restoration may seem unattainable. Unfortunately, amid the stress and hopeless feelings of a trustless relationship, many men hit the Eject button. The odds appear so stacked against them, they write off the relationship regardless of how many years have been invested.

In my counseling office, many men tell me they feel so behind the eightball when it comes to restoring trust that they don't see the point of even trying. In these cases, divorce occurs prematurely. There is very little attempt at restoration, much less the full investment of time and energy required for such a venture. It is terribly sad, because truth be told, these men don't really know if divorce has to be the final outcome.

In the shameful wake of their disclosure of a sexual failure (or, more commonly, being found out), many men can't muster the courage to look beyond the carnage of the present and glimpse the horizon of what could be a hopeful future. If these men could only see that trust building is possible. If only a man could see that someday his wife would risk her heart with him again. Someday it would be possible that she'd have more respect and adoration for him than ever before.

Building trust back in a relationship damaged by sexual integrity issues is a culmination of all the aforementioned things—and then some. It is like building a sculpture out of Legos. Some of the pieces include time, energy, planning, vision, willingness, creativity, persistence, patience, intentionality, hope, failure, and commitment. That's a lot of Legos!

Trust building is an ongoing process that consists of multiple intentional factors divinely pieced together over the course of time with a heart attitude of humility and commitment.

In reality, there is no formula for rebuilding trust. The process cannot be precisely prescribed or predicted. Trust building happens when it happens. What is required of the trust builder is to continue to faithfully place pieces into the structure, not haphazardly, but methodically. Not carelessly, but carefully.

My wife, Shelley, and I gave a talk at a MOPS (mothers of preschoolers) group recently, and one of the women asked Shelley how she knew she could trust me again. Shelley's response was simple yet incredibly complex. "I just knew," she stated.

Not rocket science, huh!

To explain, she gave an example of one of our trust-building tools: the five-minute phone call rule. This rule is a mutual agreement between us that Shelley can call me at any time and expect me to answer the phone. Should I not answer, I have a five-minute window in which to call her back. Beyond that time frame, Shelley has the right to immediately think the worst and assume I am again betraying God, her, and our relationship. Any work I've done to that point to rebuild trust is in jeopardy—and she can feel that way without apology.

The woman who asked the question looked puzzled. She didn't say anything, but the look on her face revealed skepticism that it could be that simple. She looked as if she wanted to say, "That's it? That's all you've got? A five-minute phone call rule?"

Yes—but also no. Every phone call I get from Shelley gives me an opportunity to place a Lego on our trust sculpture. Every time I pick up her call, and she verifies my whereabouts, or every time I return her call within the time window, a small element of trust is built.

Over time, combined with many other Lego-placement opportunities, trust is gradually built and restored. Shelley began to "just know" that she could trust me, because she could make out the essence and form of the trust sculpture, which we saw as safe, secure, and verifiable.

She could sense it, see it, and experience it.

More than anything, though, what enabled Shelley to begin to trust me was recognizing and accepting her source of security in someone other than me. Shelley came to terms with the reality that she would be okay even if everything in life weren't okay. In particular, even if I was not okay. Even if I was not trustworthy and never placed another Lego on our relational work of art, she would be okay.

Like Shelley, in order to change and engage the process of trust building, I, too, needed to come to terms with the truth that God was ultimately the change agent and healer. He is the true trust builder. He is the master architect and artist shaping any sculpture. If both Shelley and I lean on him for our journey of rebuilding our relationship, then neither of us must lean against each other. Because, inevitably, one of us will tire and let the other down. If we're leaning on each other for our ultimate source of strength and comfort, we will disappoint each other.

Every time.

And that can lead to a deep sense of hopelessness that has only one outcome: calling it quits.

This point cannot be overemphasized. If we are counting on our spouse to ultimately fulfill, complete, and restore us, we will be perpetually disappointed. We will long for the next relationship, which by chance might be better, easier, more fulfilling, more exciting, or more secure. But probably not. The wise King Solomon chased the next thing over and over again and came up empty. He called this "chasing after the wind" (Ecclesiastes 2:11).

If a relationship is to be restored and trust reestablished, it requires the master artist crafting the sculpture. We are simply responsible for placing the Legos. I repeat this point because there is so much confusion about what builds trust.

Speaking of confusion about what builds trust, our starting point must be to clear up some of the confusion. We must deal with some common misconceptions about trust building. Too often I find that people have a misinformed idea of how and what builds trust. It's scary to me how often I hear clients quote (sometimes unwittingly) a random television series line or a celebrity's theory on relationships, especially as it pertains to sexual integrity.

We're bombarded daily with messages about how fidelity in relationships should work. These are sitcom snapshots of how forgiveness and trust should look, and we are coached on how to respond to our spouse when things don't go well. In the unreal entertainment world, any relational damage is quickly patched up in an episode or two. If that's what you think, let me tell you straight that real life and real healing are nothing like that.

Part of the motivation for writing this book is to give husbands and wives a more accurate idea of what the process of healing trust looks like. It is long, arduous, messy, absolutely not formulaic, sometimes comical, often depressing, and always mysterious. It is a process of trial and error. Certainly there are similarities in the way people experience the rebuilding of trust, but at the end of the day, the process is *your* process.

As you embark on the journey of trust building, my hope is that this book will help you with insights and tools. I want you to understand how trust is built after it's been shattered by sexual integrity issues. I also want you to have specific examples of how to employ these tools to maximize their effectiveness. What good are tools if you don't know how to use them?

In addition, there are two other features of this book that I hope you find useful. At various points, you'll find reflection and encouragement from my wife in sections labeled "Shelley's Thoughts." These sections are designed to give you a different angle on what's required for effective trust building. I urge you to carefully read Shelley's insights and allow her input to be a voice representing your wife.

Finally, my coauthor, Stephen Arterburn—respected author, counselor, and host of the radio program *New Life Live*—offers his wisdom on the topic of rebuilding trust in a foreword, afterword, and a series of comments throughout the text that are set off as "Insight from Stephen Arterburn." You will find his thoughts both challenging and encouraging as you journey through this book.

So let's dive in. But before we begin, I want to tell you the story of a man who totally destroyed his wife's trust and then, by God's grace, slowly won it back.

That man is me.

# 2

# Trust Broken...and Restored

My story begins in a small town in Oklahoma. I grew up on thirty acres where friends and I played war in dry creek beds. I was eleven and the guys I played with were older by a couple of years. One day, after jumping into our fort and foxholes during an imaginative war game, I saw something unlike anything I had ever seen before. One of my friends had a hardcore pornographic magazine and began flipping through the pages, showing me pictures I had no category for.

I remember experiencing two distinct feelings simultaneously. First, *excitement*. Those pictures were electric, and somehow a switch flipped inside me when I saw them. They awakened something within me. Second, *guilt*. I sensed that what we were looking at was a secret and that no one should know about it. Later, at times when more magazines were shared between my friends and me, I felt like I should peek over my shoulder to be sure nobody was watching us.

Shortly after being introduced to pornography, I stumbled across it on television. I don't remember the circumstance, but late one night, while channel surfing, I found a channel with people acting out what I'd seen in the magazines. It was also around that time that I discovered masturbation and realized that it felt good when you put the two together.

Throughout my teenage years I became heavily involved with pornography and also became sexually active. When I was sixteen, the girl I was dating and her family were Christians. They talked to me often about Jesus. At the time I put up with it because I wanted to date her. I even went to a cheesy Christian youth convention where, of course, I had no interest in being except for the fact that I got to spend the weekend with her. Little did I know that God had a different plan. He spoke to me in a profound way that weekend, and I gave my life to Christ. I'll be forever grateful to my girlfriend and her family, because their prompting helped alter the course of my life. Unfortunately, becoming a Christian did not curb my sexual integrity issues. And it sure brought a new level of guilt and shame.

By the time I landed in college, I had multiple sex partners, was party to a teenage pregnancy, and habitually used pornography. *I was sexually addicted.* I didn't know it as that, and I would never have identified myself as such, but in retrospect I hated what I was doing and swore each time would be the last. But I couldn't stop.

I met Shelley at school, and by our sophomore year, I knew she was the one. She was amazing, and I saw in her a purity, authenticity, and naiveté like no one else before. None compared to her. Our relationship progressed, and we eventually got engaged. We both did a victory lap and stayed at the University of Oklahoma for five years.

During our last semester of college, Shelley lived a couple of hours away, where she was finishing an internship. I was living alone, and most of my friends had graduated the year before. I spent quite a bit of time by myself and spent ridiculous amounts of time online looking at porn. I discovered chat rooms, and in a binge episode, I engaged a woman in a lengthy conversation and we agreed to meet. But I freaked out as soon as she appeared. It took only minutes for me to swear I had made a mistake and usher her away. I told myself this was simply a close call, and that marriage would probably fix me. Besides, everyone knows that once you're married, you can have all the sex you want all the time, right?

Shelley and I graduated and got married in the same month. Things were good for about three months, but then I went back online. I picked up exactly where I left off: porn, chat rooms, and another arranged meeting. By the end of our first year of marriage, I'd met three women through the Internet. The cycle of swearing it off, doing it again, hating myself, and swearing it off again was becoming all too familiar.

At the time I was working for Arthur Andersen, an accounting and consulting firm, in Denver. And then we moved to Dallas, hoping for a fresh start. Our marriage was a wreck, and Shelley had no idea why. Shortly after the move, I was fired from Andersen because I basically stopped going to work. Instead of showing up at a client site, I would stay at home, online and acting out.

Next I worked at a mortgage company, but I had to leave that job because I was caught having an affair with a coworker. Shelley sensed that something sketchy was happening, so she asked me about it. I made up a lame story to explain why I was unreachable and lied about the affair. I told her I had "almost cheated" and then blamed her for our marital issues. I suggested that my near miss with straying was because of her—that she needed to initiate more sex, have different sex, and essentially become a different woman. She unfortunately believed me.

I took a job as a regional manager with another company, and it involved my traveling for a few weeks a month. I was a train wreck. My addiction owned me. There came a point after I took this job that things changed. Instead of trying to fit my addiction into my life, I began trying to fit my life into my addiction. Acting out became my top priority, and I scheduled flights, planned meetings, slept, awakened, and ate around opportunities to get a hit of my addiction.

Anytime I tell my story I use the same example to describe what the bottom looked like for me. It helps me to stay in touch with the absurdity of my addiction, and it reminds me that I'm not the best CEO of my life.

I would fly into a city at 7 a.m., spend the day and have dinner with the client, then check into my hotel. As I would walk in the door, I would toss my suitcase to the side, grab my computer bag, and open up my laptop. I would get online and start surfing through pornography and chatting. Around midnight or 1 a.m., I would go out and meet up with someone I had connected with over the web. At 3 or 4 a.m. I would return to my hotel, open my laptop, and start looking at porn and chatting. When the sun came up, I'd take a shower, throw on some clothes, and head back to the client's office.

That night, after dinner, I'd do the same thing all over again. I was staying up for days on end and acting out every night. By this point I was suicidal. I had prayed too many times for God to help, and too many times he seemed silent. One night I almost drove my truck off a highway. I figured it was the best way to make the horror stop. Everyone would wonder what had happened to me. Shelley would be better off without me. And no one would have to know the truth. Thank the Lord I skidded to a stop in the middle of the road. I was in shock.

Only a few weeks later I had an epiphany. I was in the shower and reflecting on my life. I saw myself through a crystal-clear lens and began to acknowledge my brokenness. My life was a wreck. My marriage was crumbling. I had lost jobs and was on track to lose another one. I hated myself. And God was a million miles away. I cried out yet again for God to show up, and in the strangest way I heard him say, "Okay." I didn't know it at the time, but he began laying a breadcrumb trail for Shelley to find out the truth.

I came home from a business trip around 10 p.m. one night, entered through the back door, greeted our lab, Astro, and made my way toward the kitchen. Within a few steps I saw Shelley sitting in the living room, and I absently said, "Hey, babe." It had become the normal play-off-any-wrongdoing comment that typified our relationship.

She responded sternly, "Sit down in that chair! You're a f—— alien to me!"

I was clueless as to what was happening. As I sat down, she asked what had happened with the woman at the mortgage company. I quickly downplayed it and lied. She demanded the truth. I found myself trying to scrounge up a vague recollection of the story I had told nine months earlier when she had confronted me then. A third time she inquired and insisted it was my last chance. In true addict fashion, I lied.

Shelley told me she had spent two hours on the phone with the woman and knew the whole story. She went into the bedroom, slamming the door behind her.

I fell facedown on the tile floor in the kitchen. I was stunned, in tears, confused, and wondering what she actually knew. I ended up sleeping on the couch that night.

I was awakened the next morning when Shelley threw a book at me, hitting me in the chest. *What to Do When Your Spouse Says "I Don't Love You Anymore"* by David Clarke is a tough-love approach to restoring a relationship after infidelity. (It helped save our marriage.)

Shelley said, "If you want to fix things, you'll have read this by the time I get home."

My speed-reading skills improved that morning, as you might imagine.

After a couple of stressful, painful, befuddled days, we decided to see the pastor who had married us. It required a six-and-a-half-hour drive to Amarillo from Dallas. That's where I came clean. During that ride I confessed to everything I could possibly think of having done, from as far back as I could remember and into my childhood.

We met with the pastor, told him my sordid story, and he labeled me a sex addict.

Strangely, I was conflicted. On the one hand, it sounded weird and deviant. On the other, it meant there was a category for monsters like me. I thought I was the only one.

Shelley heard the label as an excuse and justification.

The pastor went on to prescribe a plan for me that included accountability, church attendance, counseling, support groups, book reading, and more.

We headed back to Dallas, and I began to work the plan.

While there was relief in having a plan, it was short-lived. We were at the beginning of a really painful journey. For several months we had conversations that lasted all night. Screaming and yelling were normal for her, not me, during these all-night talks. The questions that came at me, often rapid-fire, were like questions from a test that was impossible to pass. Everything seemed hopeless.

We were in counseling twice a week during that time. It felt like the counselor was also beating me up in most of our sessions. Yet there were insights that helped me to find freedom and instructions to help me engage Shelley's pain.

The first major milestone came thirteen months later. Shelley finally decided to stay in the marriage and to forgive me. Before that, it was a coin toss. I didn't know if I would wake up to divorce papers or not. And the roller coaster of emotions that never seemed to end was so unpredictable I had no real barometer of our progress. Her commitment to the marriage and to ongoing forgiveness was huge.

Shortly after our forgiveness moment, though, it all went back to what felt like ground zero. Years later I realized the pattern and accepted that two steps forward and several steps back was normal. We dealt with and continued to deal with triggers when my past came up. It necessitated intimate conversations about past pain, reassurance, and the future.

## The Restoration Journey

A couple of years after this all began, I received a random phone call from Paul Scott (a guy I hardly knew then but have the privilege of working alongside now). We had met at a church home group and talked maybe twice. He told me God had put it on his heart to invite me to interview for a job at a ministry called Every Man's Battle. It worked out, and I left corporate America. That's a story in itself that I won't go into here. And I accepted the job without consulting Shelley. Yeah, I'm a slow learner!

Fast-forward to today. It's been an incredible ride. It took the better part of five years to feel like we were stabilized. It took seven years for Shelley to say she actually respected me. It took eight years for her to say that if we had to go through it all over again, she would still choose me. It took nine years for her to say that my sexual addiction was one of the best things that ever happened to her. My jaw hit the floor when she said that. Today, as I write this, it's a little over ten years since the mocha hit the fan. We have seen God's amazing redemption play out, and our marriage is special. We're still trying to figure out intimacy, still working through painful memories of the past, still leaning into conflict. And trust, well, trust has been and is still being restored. It's an ongoing thing, which is exactly what prompted my penning this book. This book is in so many ways a "don't do what I did" manuscript. It is the culmination of a decade of trial and error. My hope is that it will give you the courage you need to lean into the trials and make fewer errors than I did.

# PART 1

# EXCHANGING MYTHS
# FOR REALITY

# 3

# Debunking Myths

I f you want to effectively restore your wife's trust in you, it's important that you not get derailed by some common myths associated with trust building and relational restoration. The reason I want to address these things early is to wipe any wrong ideas off the foundation on which your new sculpture of trust is to be built. I don't want to throw the baby out with the bathwater on these myths—the reality is that elements of each are part of the trust-building journey—but by themselves, the eight myths we'll discuss do not rebuild trust. With each one, I'll state the myth and then explain why it needs debunking.

This exercise will help clarify your starting point for rebuilding trust. Also, I believe an understanding of these myths will help manage your expectations about the process. Many men lean on these myths to prop up their weak attempts at trust building. Your expectations need to be realistic in order to avoid severe disappointment.

## MYTH 1: TIME HEALS ALL WOUNDS AND BUILDS TRUST

The calendar will not fix damaged trust. The truth is that time alone really does not heal all wounds. If you ask victims of rape, infidelity, or abuse if time by itself has eradicated their pain, they will quickly tell you no. In fact, time doesn't even remove the memory, much less the hurt. Sure, with time, memories fade and details become fuzzy. Our recollection diminishes, and some details seem to disappear from our memory bank. But then something happens. We're triggered. Some little nuance in our day reminds us of what we've forgotten, and then we know we haven't really forgotten anything. In fact, when there has been little or no true healing, any memory of the event becomes as fresh and tangible as the day we experienced it.

Maybe it's the way someone walks or talks, a name on a sign, a character on a television show, a place mentioned in a news headline, or a billboard on our drive home. So often in my counseling work a wife says she is trying to forget the past and heal, but daily life brings her in contact with triggers such as people, places, or things that remind her of the violation of trust. Instantly, she is back at square one.

Recently a wife whose husband struggled with masturbation and had an emotional affair said, "I want to move past this stuff, but it seems like everywhere I turn, I'm reminded of infidelity and how rampant it is!"

This observation is so common. We can't live in a cave to avoid life. And moving to a faraway country is not an option for most people. Further, we really don't want to live in a faraway country or a cave. We want to be in our life but without these reminders, without all this pain. We don't want to have to escape and get away; we want *it* to go away!

I want to reframe your view of time as it pertains to this journey. Instead of looking at time as healing in itself, look at time as the context in which you find new opportunities to build trust.

Lamentations 3:22–23 says that the Lord's mercies are "new every morning." If you are trying to rebuild trust, I encourage you to look at every morning as a new beginning, a new day to seize every opportunity to build trust. Time alone will not heal your wounds. But time filled with sincere attempts to build trust—paving the way toward the future while amending the past (which we'll discuss later)—will heal your wounds.

We must be active participants in the time we have, not just observers watching time go by.

### Shelley's Thoughts

Early on, I spent a lot of my time dialing into my immediate feelings, whether good or bad. I also spent time watching and waiting on Jason...and on God. I was waiting to see if Jason would allow God to change him to be the man I knew he could be, and so I watched Jason's every move. I was also waiting on God to show me whether I should stay with Jason.

Take Away: Make use of every moment you have! Your wife is watching you!

## MYTH 2: NOT ACTING OUT AGAIN IS ALL IT TAKES TO BUILD TRUST

There certainly is some truth in this myth; it's just terribly incomplete. Not acting out again—in other words, not behaving badly, not engaging in damaging sexual activity, not doing something that violates trust again—is important. But alone it is not enough.

Not repeating bad behavior will help a spouse move away from doubt and away from always wondering when the other shoe will drop. It will help your wife to heal in terms of what she worries about day in and day out. It will also contribute to a general sense of security.

But even though these are all really good things in and of themselves, they won't draw a spouse back to trust. There is more to trust than just stopping bad behavior. In addition, there must be redemption through new, healthy behaviors. Ephesians 4:28 speaks to this:

He who has been stealing must steal no longer, but must work, doing something useful with his own hands, that he may have something to share with those in need.

The point is this: it's not enough to stop doing some bad thing; we have to begin doing a redemptive new thing. In the new thing there is something extra or in abundance. And out of our abundance we are to give to others.

Now, the text doesn't say this, and I don't want to add to the text, but think for a minute about this: if we are thieves, and someone gives to us out of his abundance, we no longer need to steal. We are beneficiaries of that person's hard work.

The same holds true for our wife. If we will stop stealing, then work, and work in such a way that we have abundance to give, our spouse will be the beneficiary. She will experience sufficiency, and she won't be compelled to steal.

Wait a minute! What would your wife be stealing?

It can come across in many ways; for instance, stealing compliments. Have you ever felt like your wife nags you to notice her? Or it could take the form of her looking for compliments from someone other than you, like an ex-boyfriend or an ex-husband. If your wife is receiving abundant compliments from you, she won't be tempted to steal affection or affirmation from other men. Or from your kids. Or from television. And she won't have to manufacture significance from you by putting you down in order to build herself up. In her darker moments, she won't have to steal your happiness by constantly bringing up the past and using it against you.

Can you see how this works?

For sure, don't act out again! That will help tremendously. But that alone will not rebuild trust. It's what you do in lieu of acting out that will build trust. Here are some questions to help jumpstart your thinking on working toward abundance:

- Will you engage rather than retreat from the relationship?
- Will you talk about feelings instead of just thoughts?
- Will you initiate hard conversations rather than wait for your wife to bring things up?

- Will you take the lead in creating a budget rather than spending frivolously?
- Will you initiate a family game night rather than a football night with your buddies?
- Will you be the one to arrange a baby-sitter for a date night rather than waiting on your wife to do it?
- Will you clean up the dishes on Thanksgiving rather than letting her stand in the kitchen for an hour washing them?
- Will you encourage her to pursue her ministry dreams rather than focus on how it inconveniences you?

You get the point. Later, in the nonnegotiables section of this book (chapters 7 through 15), you'll find several tools that will help you work toward abundance.

## Myth 3: Trust Will Be Restored When She Stops Being So Controlling

Some wives—and some husbands, too—are control freaks. Period. They can't stand to relinquish the reins to anyone, especially an unfaithful spouse. And that can be an incredible detriment to trust building. However, it is important for a wife to protect her heart from being violated again, so at least for a time, she needs to feel she can exert some control. A wife's fear in the beginning is having her heart ripped out and stomped on again. So she has to protect herself and put some guardrails in place to maintain her security.

For example, there is a place for Internet filtering and reporting, for GPS phone tracking, for following you around, for snooping through your e-mail, for locking down the computer and the television, and so forth. In the beginning of the restorative process, some of these are appropriate. Some, however, are inappropriate, but they will happen anyway. Some are necessary to give your wife a semblance of safety.

Usually, prior to disclosure, there has already been some level of control. A wife has tried to employ some form of heart protection that may feel like mothering or baby-sitting to the husband (and often to both spouses). She doesn't want to do it, she doesn't feel good about doing it, but she is compelled to do it in order to keep her heart safe.

Many recovery circles call this codependency or co-addiction. But I don't use these labels. While a *co-* state may be present to some degree, such labels can be applied usually only later in the process. In the beginning, it is too difficult to distinguish between self-protection and codependency. The difficulty is exponentially increased when pain is inflicted by continued acting-out behavior. If your wife prior to your failure was controlling to the point that you believed it was a core issue in your marriage, you must understand that now is *not* the time to bring it up. If ever there was a time to try to fix an issue like this between you, this isn't it!

If you insist that her alleged control issues must be dealt with now, then you can forget about rebuilding trust. I counsel many men who take this position. They cannot see their own issues because they are in denial and want to focus only on their wife's issues. This is just shifting the blame, much like what Adam did to Eve in the garden: "The woman you gave me made me do it." Rather than deal with our own junk, it seems easier and less painful to focus on someone else's.

As a side note, let me share what I often see in the folks I try to help. Where there is a wife who is overbearing and controlling, there is usually deep insecurity and fear. The husband points to the controlling nature of his wife and insists that she needs to deal with it, get counseling for it, take medication, and/or get over it. But when I ask these husbands to consider how much of their married life they've spent helping their wife experience a sense of security, they often respond defensively with examples of financial provision and stability.

While financial security is important to many wives, money is not a re-placement for their heart. Many wives say they would rather take fewer vaca-tions and have a smaller house in exchange for feeling emotionally connected, secure, and cared for. I believe that the controlling attitude and posture of many wives is a response to the lack of emotional and relational security they feel from their husband.

If, as a husband, you strive to love your wife as Christ loved the church and surrender your rights to her, and there is still a deeply controlling nature, then the issue lies on the other side of the fence. This is something she will have to deal with as the Holy Spirit leads her. But you can't be the judge of that. Not now, at least.

### Shelley's Thoughts

I definitely have a tendency to control, especially when my life feels out of control. This was a really big issue in our marriage before I found out the ugly truth about Jason's secret life. I think I hated being the controller just as much as Jason hated feeling controlled. Neither of us realized that the lack of secu-rity (a.k.a. out of control) in our relationship was the primary driver for me.

It came as quite a shock when at some point we stepped back and realized the control in our relationship wasn't as perva-sive as it had been in the past. (It was also quite a relief to me!)

Did the control issues go completely away? Unfortunately, no. It is something I've continued to struggle with, although to a much lesser degree.

Take Away: Here is some good news: being in a stable and secure relationship with Jason has been a huge part of the reason I have felt okay in working on myself, including my controlling tendencies.

So if you feel like your wife is controlling you, I encourage you to do two things. First, surrender your right to control. Isn't that ironic? You want her to stop being so controlling, so you try your best to control her. Shelve your entitlement to be the decision maker, especially on things pertaining to the healing process. And please, don't play the "head of the house" card. You relinquished that position when you chose to behave in a way that violated your wife's heart.

Second, focus on security. Or maybe better to say, *providing* security. Investigate what your wife needs to feel safe emotionally, physically, and mentally. Yes, her ultimate security must be found in God, but that doesn't mean you can't be a conduit of his grace to her.

## INSIGHT FROM STEPHEN ARTERBURN

### Admit Your Powerlessness

There are a few things that will help you stay focused during the process of regaining trust. The first is the concept of powerlessness. I did not write "helplessness," which is something quite different. You are not helpless. But when you admit, confess, and believe you are powerless over an addiction to lust or affairs or whatever form of sexual gratification you choose, you are building strength into your life and into your wife's life. If you start to believe you are moving beyond feeling powerless, in fact, your strength will lessen and your vulnerability to relapse will intensify.

Your life took a major turn for the better when you first admitted you were powerless to turn this around on your own. It was your moment of greatest strength since the point when you started down the path toward disruption, dependency, and addiction. Every day you wake up and reassert your powerlessness, you make yourself stronger, and your wife will notice your strength. And her security will increase along with her trust in you.

# 4

# The "He Must Not Love Me" Myth

As counterintuitive as it may seem, men rarely commit sexual betrayal because of a lack or loss of love for their wife. Hardly ever does a man who has fallen sexually sit in my office and say that he doesn't love his wife anymore. It happens on occasion, but even then it often is not true. Usually when a husband expresses that he doesn't love his wife, he is making a statement about his own shame. He is grasping at straws and trying to make sense of his own behavior. This particular logic says, "If I am willing to hurt her this badly, over and over again, then I must not love her." For some guys it's easier to stomach the explanation of "falling out of love" or "I must not have truly loved her anyway" than it is to acknowledge their own mean, evil, destructive sin. It is incredibly difficult for men to accept and own the reality that the people we love the most are the people we've hurt the worst.

## Myth 4: He Wouldn't Do This If He Really Loved Me

The issue of acting out sexually has little to do with whether or not a husband loves his wife. It also has next to nothing to do with whether or not he loves Jesus. The faulty assumption is that something outside the person will motivate him to change. Our reality is that consequences are a poor long-term motivator. Likewise, positive outcomes or benefits are also poor long-term motivators. You can repeatedly tell an addict that he'll blow up his life if he keeps acting out, and he still won't change. You'll get the same result if you tell him how great his life will be if he gets into recovery. Such tactics don't work.

What brings about authentic change is a mysterious, dynamic interaction between our soul and the triune God. Until someone who is living a life of sin decides he can no longer bear living that way, nothing will change. The scale must tip in a way that the pain of staying the same outweighs the pain of change. In recovery circles, they say we must get sick and tired of being sick and tired. Without this realization, things may change on the surface, but true, deep character change will remain elusive.

Tying this back to our topic, we can substitute any external force into the myth, and it will remain just that: a myth.

- He would stop if he loved Jesus and went to church more.
- He wouldn't do this if he loved our kids more.
- He would be a man of integrity if we didn't live in such a sex-saturated culture.
- He wouldn't have done this if he had not been abused.

When the scale tips and the motivation becomes internal, then authentic change can occur. Until then, love is not the issue. "Igniting the old flame," as some wives try to do, will only serve to kick the can of recovery farther down the street and delay dealing with reality.

## COMPARTMENTALIZATION

The debunking of this myth requires a brief overview of compartmentalization. Please know this is simply an explanation, not an excuse for a man's sexual acting out.

Men who commit sexual betrayal, especially those who are sexually addicted, are incredibly adept at compartmentalizing their behavior. Picture a closet wall with shelves from top to bottom, wall to wall. Each shelf holds as many shoeboxes as possible. Every box has a label that can easily be seen and read: Home, Family, Work, Hobbies, Addictions, Sexual Sin, God, and so on. These boxes represent the fragmented, compartmentalized mind of a man consumed with sexual sin. Each box holds areas of his life that ideally would be intermingled. But with an unhealthy person, these areas are isolated so that one doesn't spill over into another.

Picture the very top shelf. On the far left side is the box marked Family. This box contains the memories of the wedding day, shared assets like a house and bank accounts, kids' birthday parties, family vacations, dinners with relatives, and Christmas mornings. It holds dreams of life together and the "happily ever after." It also holds love, commitment, empathy, security, provision, care, concern, and the other raw materials that make up the fabric of a marital relationship. At a time when a man is doing family life, for example, on Christmas morning, he slides this box off the shelf and pops off the lid. He is fully immersed in the contents (not to be confused with being fully present in the moment) and thus not digging around any of the other boxes. His mind is on his family and the festivities of unwrapping gifts, putting together toys, finding batteries, and cooking breakfast. When he is finished with the Family box, he puts all the contents back in, places the lid firmly on the top, and returns it to its place on the top shelf.

On the bottom shelf, in the far right-hand corner, is a box labeled Sexual Sin. This box contains the destructive, painful, shame-filled, and exciting elements of his addiction. When a man pulls this box off the shelf and dumps out the contents, he is totally engrossed by them. Whether the box contains pornography, masturbation, strip club visits, an affair—all of which could be indicative of a sexual addiction—his attention is solely focused on its contents.*

---

\* For further discussion of "fractional addiction," see Stephen Arterburn and Fred Stoeker, *Every Man's Battle* (Colorado Springs, CO: WaterBrook, 2000), 30.

By the way, some men describe a feeling of tunnel vision when they head toward acting out, as if they can see nothing else but the next high. This is a function of compartmentalization and, metaphorically, digging around inside this box. What's important to understand is that when a man is preoccupied with his Sexual Sin box, he is completely out of touch with and disconnected from his Family box. It's as if when he is in one box, he is literally detached from all the others.

A wife will ask how her husband could commit the act of betrayal without thinking about her or the family. This is how: men compartmentalize their lives to the point where the singular focus of one area is all encompassing and becomes a barrier to his commingling the other compartments. The boxes are distinct and separate; there is very little overlap. When we're in one box, we aren't in another. There are rare occasions when, even though a man is mesmerized with the contents of his Sexual Sin box, a moment of clarity and conscience will prompt him to take a quick glance at the Family box. For a brief, fleeting moment, he'll think, *I shouldn't be in this box. I should pick up all these pieces, close up the box, and throw it in the trash. I should completely get it out of the closet. For good...*

But the contents grab his attention again and redirect him, so he ignores what he has seen. Addictive, compulsive, coping, self-preserving tendencies prevail, and he continues in shame-bound denial. Once he has acted out and no longer needs what the Sexual Sin box offers, he'll quickly scoop up the contents, replace the lid, and return it to the shelf. He might not even think about that box until the addiction beckons again.

When a wife hears me share this closet metaphor, she'll say something about how frustrated the whole thing makes her. She'll say that compartmentalization sounds like an excuse. Even Shelley had this opinion when she was proofreading this section! She felt a little frustrated, like I was providing an escape clause or something for the men who commit betrayal. It seems to tap a nerve in wives.

That's okay. I'm not writing this to fix it or make it feel better, nor even to make a husband's betrayal more palatable. I simply want everyone to be informed and to understand. There is a small part of me that hopes a wife will process this information in a way that decreases her inclination to vilify her husband. It does not apply to every wife, but some see their husband as a terrible monster who has deliberately stripped away their dignity and whose evil intent is to inflict perpetual wounds. Chances are, this is just not the case.

Anyway, from this quick overview of compartmentalization, it's safe to say that the boxes are self-soothing, coping strategies that men use to deal with life. The fragmented mind of a sexually addicted man often finds its origin in his childhood. For myriad reasons, the child needed and developed distinct boxes, each with its own set of rules, regulations, and relationships in order to make sense of or deal with the pain and confusion in his world.

We all compartmentalize to some extent. For example, we each have a unique set of parameters that guide our speech and behavior when we are at an important business dinner versus a meal at home. Different rules apply to our conduct when we are at a funeral as opposed to a wedding. While we all have some compartmentalization techniques that help us appropriately navigate life, a man who commits sexual betrayal has more distinct and defined containers and stronger dividers between them. This facilitates his ability to willingly commit such hurtful acts and inflict immeasurable damage to his marriage and other family relationships.

Compartmentalization is not nearly as big an issue for women. They typically don't operate this way. Most women think holistically. They have fewer distinct boxes in their closets, so to speak, and many of them are interconnected. What goes on in one container affects others, because they are interwoven. As such, almost every wife I talk to says she could never imagine herself behaving in such hurtful ways and with total disregard for her husband and children.

Remember that the root word of *integrity* is *integer,* a whole number. It is not divisible nor disjointed. Thus striving for integrity means working toward integrating all the compartments. Extending the metaphor of the closet of boxes, integrity is a process by which all the boxes are removed from the shelves and dumped in the middle of the floor, where all the pieces commingle. The contents of one box mix with the contents of the other boxes. Work melds with Family. Home gets intermixed with Hobbies. Sexual Sin is dealt with because it's in the same pile as the God and Church boxes. In fact, this is one of the primary drivers for encouraging men to commit to full disclosure. The deconstructing of the boxes that hold all our secrets is a prerequisite for integration within ourselves, with our wives, and with God.

# 5

# The More and Different Sex Myth

There is a painful, false belief woven into the fabric of our culture that permeates the thinking of almost everyone I see at my office. A surprisingly high number of counselors and pastors believe this myth too! Yet it is incredibly damaging to the man who struggles sexually. It is equally as damaging to the wife who believes it.

It's simply not true that more or more exciting sex will keep a man from wandering and curb his sexual acting out. In fact, in most cases, it makes things worse. Why is this so?

## MYTH 5: HAVING MORE OR DIFFERENT SEX WILL CURB HIS ACTING OUT

This myth is so damaging for men because it perpetuates both the deficient emotional intimacy issues that underlie acting out as well as the neural chemistry of acting out. Increasing frequency of sexual intercourse with one's wife usually serves only to create an expanded context for acting out. Now, in addition to a computer, a hotel room, an office, or a strip club being the place where sexual misconduct occurs, it also takes place in the marriage bed. The husband's view of his wife changes from seeing her as a beautiful child of God and dearly treasured companion to viewing her as another object available for vaginal masturbation. Does that sound harsh? It should, because it is harsh.

This is what happens, though, when we use our wife for sexual gratification devoid of any aspect of deep, loving emotional intimacy. Moreover, when a wife agrees to do sex differently, meaning more "exciting" or "exotic" by trying different positions, clothing, conversation, or implements, she simply becomes an equivalent of the husband's debilitating porn, a personal prostitute—and neither husband nor wife consciously perceives this. To an addict, this request to his wife is nothing more than vicariously clicking his computer mouse. His wife becomes an object to be manipulated for his desire, not to connect with her soul, not to honor God, not to show love, not to create a bond unlike any other on the planet. Instead, simply to get off.

Transforming one's wife into an object for gratification is cruel, demeaning, and, frankly, a slap in God's face. Objectification takes the gift of a wife who has been generously joined to a husband for mutual benefit and development and crassly converts her into a thing to gratify his selfish desires.

It is pertinent to note the neural chemical aspect of seeking more exciting sex or exotic sex. Other books delve into the details of this, so I'll keep it fairly brief here. A host of chemicals are released in the brain during sexual activity, including dopamine, epinephrine, adrenaline, and serotonin. For the sake of this discussion, the primary chemical driver in sexual addiction is dopamine, which motivates the pursuit of novelty and excitement.

Invia Betjoseph, a friend and an Every Man's Battle Workshop counselor, describes dopamine as gasoline in an eight-cylinder car engine. Sexual addiction and acting out affects the brain in such a way that the amount of dopamine released into the brain is excessive. It floods the engine. Over time, the brain loses calibration, and the behavior necessary to satisfy the urge for dopamine intensifies. With each flooding of dopamine, the person is pushed toward achieving a bigger and bigger high. Thus, addiction escalation occurs.

As Invia says, the addict ends up confusing intensity for intimacy. Asking his wife to heighten the sexual arousal experience serves only to strengthen the unhealthy neural pathways that perpetuate the addiction. Neither the addict nor his wife wants this outcome.

I think it's worth repeating that I'm speaking here to a husband and wife whose relationship has been damaged by sexual betrayal, and I'm specifically addressing a marriage in which the husband struggles with sexual integrity issues. Engaging in heightened sexual arousal and experimenting in the bedroom can be perfectly fine and, in fact, create a new level and type of intimacy for a couple whose sexual trust has not been broken. But if you're reading this book and trying to restore trust in your relationship in the aftermath of sexual betrayal, you cannot risk reinforcing your old addictive thought patterns. The neural networks associated with those thought patterns affect intimacy on every level, maintain self-preservation, activate consequence-avoidance techniques (perpetuating further lies), and are connected to the kind of compartmentalization that allows someone to live a duplicitous life.

## A WIFE'S DILEMMA

For wives who buy into this myth, the resulting problems can be as bad as those of their husband. A wife wants to be wanted. In general, she wants to be pursued and doted on. In the beginning of the trust-building process, she may want her husband to keep his distance. At some point, though, she will want him to pursue her again. Sometimes wives believe that if they were more sexually active with their husband, it would offset his sexual acting out. As with all myths, there is a sliver of truth here, but the reality is that a wife's sexier behavior may curb his acting out *outside* the bedroom, but it won't change what happens in his heart and mind *inside* the bedroom. His character and attitude as it pertains to his sexuality will remain unchanged.

Ultimately, what we're shooting for is not just stopping his acting out and having more sex within the marriage. The goal is to experience sexuality in a way that honors God and each other. We're aiming for an experience of knowing and being known so intimately that it bonds our souls together.

A wife who acts on a belief that more or different sex will prevent further sexual indiscretions will only prolong her husband's core problem. She will delay his healing and, unfortunately, hurt herself too. This occurs in three ways.

First, the wife can become a personal prostitute in exchange for personal security. The currency she is paid is the semblance of security that her heart won't be violated again. Wives often report feeling backed into a corner on this one, because they feel forced to choose between two bad options. On the one hand, they might not feel the emotional or spiritual intimacy necessary for authentic sexual engagement, yet they still feel compelled to oblige sexually. They end up allowing their bodies to be used for their husband's gratification. It's worth noting that many wives report that they struggle with thoughts about when, how, and with whom their husband has done the same thing. They ask, "Did he touch her this way?" "Did he say these things to another woman?" "Did he look for pictures of women doing these acts?" Their minds become a mental prison cell, and the torturer is their husband. On the other hand, should the wife choose not to engage sexually, the risk is that her husband will act out again, thus violating her heart and sense of security.

So, husband, my question to you is, Do you really want to put your wife in this position?

This also applies to wives who feel more pressure to initiate sexual activity. I often hear from husbands about a disparity between levels of initiation. "I just wish she would initiate more often," they say. I used to say that too! Then I realized that the problem wasn't Shelley's willingness to initiate; it was her lack of desire to initiate. Ouch! The reality was that I didn't love her in ways that would prompt her to want to initiate anything. I had to own that fact about our relationship. Perhaps you should too.

The second problem with a wife who buys into the "more sex will help" myth is that if she's asked to behave in ways she isn't comfortable with in the bedroom, this can translate into a loss of her sense of self. In other words, she has to be or do something other than who she really is. This is not the picture of a marriage where each partner is seeking to honor the uniqueness of a God-created individual.

It pains me to hear men say they are disappointed with their wife's willingness to be exciting in the bedroom. Too often they are communicating a secret, almost subconscious reality. Their idea of what should go on in the bedroom is tainted by what they've seen in porn! If you want your wife to behave, move, sound, and look like the scripted, artificial, manufactured, airbrushed images you've seen on-screen, you will be perpetually disappointed. And she will always feel like she is playing second fiddle to your unrealistic fantasies, resulting in a wound of inadequacy.

Wives don't want to have to compete with that stuff, nor should they. Your wife wants to be honored and cherished for her heart, mind, character, personality, sense of humor, love for the Lord, and other qualities. And then for her body—maybe.

Now it is only prudent to pull back the curtain and expose another biblical justification behind a myth. Quoted ad nauseam by Christian sex addicts, the following lines of Scripture are easily twisted and misconstrued. I can't imagine what Jesus would say if he were to confront someone in sexual sin and these verses were tossed at him as justification for sexual immorality.

Now for the matters you wrote about: It is good for a man not to marry. But since there is so much immorality, each man should have his own wife, and each woman her own husband. The husband should fulfill his marital duty to his wife, and likewise the wife to her husband. The wife's body does not belong to her alone but also to her husband. In the same way, the husband's body does not belong to him alone but also to his wife. Do not deprive each other except by mutual consent and for a time, so that you may devote yourselves to prayer. Then come together again so that Satan will not tempt you because of your lack of self-control. I say this as a concession, not as a command. (1 Corinthians 7:1–6)

Let me first frame the context for what the apostle Paul has written here. This is a response to a letter from the church in Corinth with questions about what it should look like to honor God in their culture. Mind you, Corinth was a lascivious crossroads where different people, cultures, and religious practices intersected. It was a sex-saturated society where "worship" at some temples took the form of sex with prostitutes. So the scene is one where, instead of guitars and drums or pipe organ and a choir, instead of singing, dancing, raised hands, and hymns, it's a bunch of people having sex. As new believers trying to find their way, the Corinthian Christians asked their church father, Paul, about the dos and don'ts of interacting with the culture around them.

While we don't have a copy of the letter from the Corinthians to Paul, especially the part pertaining to sexual immorality, I imagine it might have said something like this:

Paul, as believers in Jesus, we know our lives should look different from the culture around us. However, there is one particular area we are struggling with: sex. See, having sex is how we worshiped false gods. Now that we follow the one true God, if we have sex, are we sinning? If we engage in sexual activity, aren't we pledging allegiance to those old, false gods again?

In response, Paul in 1 Corinthians 7 addresses sexual immorality by talking about how important it is to remain pure and to treat sex and our body with respect. In this very specific response to the Corinthian dilemma, he clearly begins to construct the container within which sexual engagement is appropriate: the marriage covenant. But here is where we can get sideways if we're not careful. Paul's direct comments are regarding sex, but the spirit of his total message is about idol worship. He is trying to affirm their commitment to each other sexually while also cautioning them against the temptation to revert to their old ways. Here's a reframing of his message in laymen's terms:

Guys, good question. I appreciate your heart for the truth and for authentic worship. Yes! By all means, have sex with your wife or husband. It's a good thing, a God thing! It is designed to be a wonderful soul-connecting experience between the two of you within which the one true God is glorified. And don't deprive each other by withholding sex. The temptation to return to worshiping false gods is great, and the temple prostitutes are always available. If a husband and wife both agree to take a break from sex, they should be committed to deepening their relationship with God during that time.

Now, this is where it gets misconstrued. Here is how Paul's message is often interpreted by the husbands I counsel in my office:

Yes, sex in your marriage is good. In fact, it is a requirement. It is part of the package. You are entitled to it, and you can demand it as you see fit. Should your spouse not be interested, she is withholding from you, thus she is sinning. In your state of deprivation, you will probably be tempted to act out sexually. And you have a right to. If you give in to sexual temptation, it is her fault for not being available.

Do you really think Paul is saying, "You aren't culpable for your sin"? I'm not saying a wife who deprives her husband sexually is in the right, nor that she won't have to deal with Jesus on the matter. What I am saying is that we are responsible for our sexual sin. No amount of sin on someone else's part is justification for sin on our part. No matter how bad our marriage may be, if we act out sexually, that's our choice and responsibility. No matter how sexless a marriage is, if we sin sexually, that choice is on us.

The third problem for a wife regarding the "more sex" myth is that she may have to manufacture pursuit, which feels very patronizing. Many wives end up losing themselves, or at least a sense of themselves, when they begin to act out sexual desire for their husband.

Manufacturing pursuit means a wife must somehow contrive a situation or circumstance that results in sex, thus mitigating her husband's acting out. She may do things or be someone other than who she authentically is in order to satisfy her husband sexually.

This is what that looked like at our house. Shelley confronted me about an affair. I manipulated her and lied about the information she had. A few days later I told her that I had "almost" cheated and that it was her fault. The truth was that I was having an affair and was looking for any reason to justify and rationalize my behavior rather than accept full responsibility. As such, I targeted Shelley with my excuses and manipulated her into owning them. I said that she wasn't sexy enough, especially in the bedroom. She donned this burden and set out to rectify her alleged problem in an attempt to please me.

She began shopping at stores she otherwise would never have shopped at. She began wearing lingerie, which was out of the ordinary for her. She began dressing in ways that were more revealing and immodest. She tried to become someone she wasn't, someone she never wanted to be. But she was willing to "spice it up" to save our marriage and mitigate the risk of my acting out and destroying her heart again.

Do you see what a disgusting, disrespectful way this is to treat another person? Would you or I like to be treated this way?

Shelley ended up disliking herself, and all her efforts yielded absolutely zero in terms of changing me. Instead, she became bitter and resentful, which created a greater relational distance between us.

And I was becoming more entrenched in my sin.

## INSIGHT FROM STEPHEN ARTERBURN

### Surrender

I have heard the mantra "one day at a time" so much that it has become part of my existence. It is so simple but also so difficult to live by. The key is daily surrender. Every day I have to surrender my will and my wants to God. I have to humble myself before him and ask him to have his way with me and my life while I die to my own agenda. That kind of surrender is not easy. Yet it is the foundation for victory. You yield to God, and he brings the victory.

"Your will, not mine" is a great daily motto that takes us from defeat to victory. In fact, each time we are willing to surrender our will to the will of God or the needs of another, it is in itself a victory. Fill your life with daily moments of surrender, and you will stay on a path to victory that glorifies God.

# 6

# Spiritual Myths

Many wives are the victims of spiritual abuse. There, I said it. Out loud. Or rather, typographically out loud. They are the victims of spiritual abuse by husbands and pastors.

It is incredibly disappointing to hear when folks have visited their pastor for help in the wake of betrayal and walked away more hurt, confused, and discouraged. Just two weeks ago I heard the story again in my office. This couple talked to a pastor at their church and discussed the husband's infidelity. The pastor's response was to tell the wife that she needs to be mindful of "taking care of herself" so as to keep her husband attracted to her. I cringe as I write this. Unfortunately, reports like this are not rare. I also regularly hear about a pastor's feedback that is geared toward forgiveness. The story goes that if the hurt spouse will simply forgive the betrayer, their relationship will heal. While true on some level, this is *way* oversimplified and creates an enormous burden for the hurt spouse. More on this in Myth 7.

If you are a pastor reading this or you know a pastor who could benefit from some guidance in this area, the chapters ahead will give you a great framework to begin helping. For more pastoral resources please visit my website, www.redemptiveliving.com.

## Myth 6: Prayer Alone or More Prayer Will Build Trust

Let me start by reassuring you that I'm not devaluing prayer. Prayer is absolutely essential. No question. But when it comes to restoring trust, prayer without a plan is a recipe for disaster.

My father-in-law often recounts an old adage: if you fail to plan, you plan to fail. I see that play out often in the lives of husbands seeking help with their relationship. More prayer in itself does not constitute a plan. Please don't misunderstand me. While prayer may be the only lifeline you have to navigate the course before you, you cannot pray your way out of something you *behaved* your way into. You have to pray *and* act.

As a husband, if you insist that your spouse needs to pray more for her own healing or for the healing of the relationship, you're probably doing more harm than good. Many Christian men do this. They talk about how their walk with God is of primary importance, which sounds good. And they say that they're powerless to heal anything, which also sounds good. Thus, they imply, it's up to their wife to do her own business with God for healing her heart and the relationship.

While it may be true that wives need to do their own business with God, it won't do any good to point that out. *She already knows this.* And from her perspective, it looks more like her husband is shirking his responsibility and blatantly disregarding her heart than doing anything godly.

She needs to see you work on regaining trust as if it *all* depends on you. Asking her to pray for her healing is not helpful. Your being in prayer for her healing—combined with your working your butt off to win her back—*that's* helpful.

I urge you to pray hard for God to empower you to follow through on the work that is ahead of you. Pray for healing. Pray for redemption. Pray for God to develop perseverance in your character. Pray for your wife and her journey toward forgiveness. Pray for God's comfort for the others you've hurt.

And don't forget that prayer without action will come up short. This is what James 2:19–20 (MSG) says about this:

> Do I hear you professing to believe in the one and only God, but then observe you complacently sitting back as if you had done something wonderful? That's just great. Demons do that, but what good does it do them? Use your heads! Do you suppose for a minute that you can cut faith and works in two and not end up with a corpse on your hands?

## MYTH 7: TRUST WILL BE RESTORED WHEN SHE DECIDES TO FORGIVE

The subject of forgiveness is explosive, controversial, intensely personal, and warrants a book of its own. And they're out there. Any bookstore will offer a considerable selection. Forgiveness is designated theologically and psychologically as an essential element in healing. However, with so much emphasis on forgiveness, it can become an end in itself. And for many marriages, unfortunately, it is the end. How can that be?

At times in a relationship where a trust violation has occurred, an inappropriate emphasis is placed on forgiveness as the primary goal and then moving past the hurt. Forgiveness is a good thing, but alone it does not build trust. Rather, it is one element that contributes to an environment that helps reestablish trust.

I have talked with too many men who believe that if their wife would just forgive them, trust would return to the relationship. This is faulty, easy-out, immediate gratification. And irresponsible thinking to boot. Many men convince themselves that this is the key to self-preservation. The logic goes like this: if my wife forgives me, she'll stop being hurt and angry; thus, she'll stop being so mean and taking it out on me. Give me a break! What this line of thought reveals is incredible selfishness. Husband, listen to me! Your wife's forgiveness is for her—not you.

And if you think that just because there has been forgiveness the anger is gone, you're going to be disappointed. When her anger pops up after she has forgiven you, you'll be surprised and likely respond defensively, which will only create more angst, hurt, and sadness. Allow your wife's forgiveness process to be her own. Release it as a requirement for trust building.

Unfortunately, some wives believe this myth, that trust will be restored as soon as they forgive their husband. They believe that their unwillingness to forgive is blocking any restoration of trust. And truth be told, in some cases it is a block. But more often, there can be authentic forgiveness by the violated party, but if there's no true repentance and change on the violator's part, trust will remain elusive.

Forgiveness on its own is incredibly difficult for a person whose trust has been violated. When forgiveness becomes the focal point of trust building, the forgiver becomes the one with the burden. The onus shifts off the violator and onto the forgiver.

Realize that this backs the forgiver into a corner. *If I am to trust, then I have to forgive. If I don't trust, it's because I haven't forgiven. If I don't forgive, then I won't be able to trust; thus, my marriage won't heal. So I must be the problem!*

No wife wants to be in that position and under that much pressure, especially when she's grieving what feels like the death of a relationship. If you are trying to rebuild trust, rather than highlight your wife's lack of forgiveness, focus on being forgivable. Think about that. What does it mean to be forgivable?

Being forgivable means you behave in a manner that makes it easier for your wife to do what is seemingly impossible. Remember, her forgiveness isn't for you—it's for her. It means operating with a contrite, humble spirit. You have to communicate gently and with tenderness. Put yourself in her shoes and consider what would make the journey easier for her. Would you be more inclined to forgive someone who is humble and tender, or someone who is arrogant, defensive, and abrasive? Realize too that the more you exhibit those latter traits, the more there is to forgive. In other words, the whole process becomes more difficult because you are compounding the pain. The words of Psalm 51:17 are fitting here:

> The sacrifices of God are a broken spirit;
>> a broken and contrite heart,
>> O God, you will not despise.

A broken and contrite heart is hard to despise. Remember, her forgiveness isn't for you—it's for her. If your commitments to live with integrity and to improve your character are solely predicated on your wife's forgiveness, you will be the one in the wrong. Rebuilding trust requires you to be forgivable, regardless of whether she is willing to forgive.

## MYTH 8: GOD WILL MIRACULOUSLY DELIVER YOU FROM YOUR SEXUAL STRUGGLE AND YOUR MARRIAGE FROM THIS PAIN

Over the years I've talked to thousands of people about this struggle. To date I've found only two individuals who claim to know a person who has been miraculously delivered from sexual temptations. And I don't believe them!

You hear it regularly about drugs and alcohol. One day someone comes to know the Lord, he prays a prayer, and he has a dramatic turnaround or even just wakes up different one morning. He never wants to do drugs again. I regularly talk to guys who have had decades of sobriety, and this is how it began for them. I believe God miraculously delivers people from some addictions. But with sexual addictions, God doesn't seem to perform immediate cures. Can he? Yes. Does he? In my opinion, not often. I am skeptical. Let me explain.

Sexual addiction is much more similar to food addiction than substance abuse. Some addiction characteristics certainly overlap: hiding, lying, cover-ups. Both sexual and substance addictions have damaging effects on work, relationships, money, spiritual journeys, and a general sense of well-being. Escalation occurs in both situations; both addicts will search for more and more ways of acting out to get high. Withdrawal symptoms follow when the addiction is ended for both scenarios, and there is a painful, strange grieving process that addicts go through over the loss of their addiction.

If we look at the recovery process, we see similarities as well. The process of rewiring the brain toward wholeness and holiness is a long-term effort. Forming healthy habits, defining helpful boundaries, understanding root causes, and being part of a support system all find their place in the recovery journey. However, this is where things start to change and sex begins to align more with food.

Consider one of the key remedies for substance abuse: ceasing use of the substance. To find freedom from a food addiction, do we stop eating entirely? Does freedom from a sexual addiction mean that we stop being sexual? I hope neither of these are true! No, instead we take a very natural, God-given aspect of our humanity that we have confused, misused, and abused and learn to engage it in a healthy, God-honoring way. Recovery isn't about finding sobriety so much as it is about sanctification. I see too many men who end up going into recovery from their addiction only to become addicted to recovery. They make recovery and meetings their entire life rather than make it become part of a bigger life that grows closer to Christ daily.

Now, back to deliverance. When I hear people say they are praying for deliverance, I ask from what?

"From sexual sin."

"From temptation?"

"Yes."

"Why?"

While this can turn into a circular conversation, I try to help the person understand what he is asking for and why. It boils down to wanting deliverance from temptation so as not to struggle with the resulting sexual sin.

But what if God doesn't want to take away sexual temptation? What if we could see the playbook in God's hands and realize that perhaps sexual temptation is yet another way he longs to develop our character and reliance on him? Temptation isn't a sin; it's what we do with it that can result in sin. And like Jesus, when he was tempted, we have options. We can choose our own road to instant gratification and pleasure, or we can lean into God, practice faith, and allow him to be enough for us.

In effect, what many men pray for is counterproductive. They end up asking God to toss out his playbook and go with their game plan. The defining characteristic of our plan, as humans, is that it makes the journey of sanctification less painful. It takes away elements of faith and mystery and replaces them with control and logic. Maybe, if we allow our mind and heart to go there, sexual temptation is a gift.

To be clear, the destruction and devastation caused on this planet by people acting on sexual temptation is not a gift. It is a tragedy. But it no longer has to be a tragedy in your life. I doubt God is going to miraculously deliver you from sexual temptation—for your own good.

## FINAL THOUGHTS ON MYTHS

In part 1, I wanted to speak explicitly to a handful of myths associated with trust building. As I indicated earlier, I don't want to rail on these things. However, I do want to put them into proper perspective and thus appropriately manage your expectations during the healing process. Too many couples show up at my office with a skewed view of what will actually help them. They are reeling from the damage caused by the husband's sexual integrity issues, and they are reaching for something that makes sense and gives them hope.

Some of these myths can fit the bill. Well-meaning people, who haven't a clue how to understand their pain or their wife's pain, will fall back on these myths. Don't buy it! Avoid additional disappointment!

Instead, send all such comments through a filter of truth and understanding, knowing that while these myths are somewhat true, they are not complete truth. Now we are ready to go to work on rebuilding trust.

# PART 2

# THE NONNEGOTIABLES
# OF TRUST BUILDING

# 7

# Spiritual Commitment

Now that we've cleared the deck of some potentially harmful myths, it's time to give you some tangible, well-explained tools to begin building trust back into your marriage.

These items are nonnegotiables, meaning that if they aren't present or if they're deficient, it will be incredibly difficult for your relationship to be restored. If you want to give yourself and your spouse the best chance at redemption, you need to be intentional about each of these items.

Before we explore these tools, I need to describe two caveats concerning these nonnegotiables. First, none of the items in this section are worthy of a pat on your back. Here's what I mean. Often men shift gears from being dishonest to being honest and immediately expect a high-five from their wife.

A wife is usually only somewhat enthused—if at all—because the reality is that her husband is finally doing what he should have been doing all along. So what's the big deal? Does that make sense?

I compare it to my son Truman when he was four years old. We were teaching him to complete a task the first time we asked him, without complaint or pushback. These were simple things like getting dressed, brushing his teeth, climbing in bed, and picking up his shoes. For example, after asking him to get ready for the day by taking off his pajamas and putting on his clothes, he'd ask, "Do I get a treat once I get my clothes on?" My answer, maybe too sarcastically, was, "Of course not!" He was asking for a treat for something he should have been doing anyway. It's not as though I asked him to do something out of the ordinary or in addition to what he was already supposed to do. And yet he expected a reward for it. Of course, he had an excuse—he was only four years old.

Yet many men in the trust-building process operate the same way. For example, a husband will express to me his frustration that his wife is angry and bitter toward him. He'll say something like, "I'm not [fill in the blank: looking at porn, cheating, visiting strip clubs, and so forth] anymore, so she should be happy with me!" Or, "I'm not [fill in the blank], so it would be nice to get a little respect and appreciation from her." Or, "It's been a year since I [fill in the blank], and I expect her to [fill in the blank]."

I hope you see the sense of entitlement and childishness in these statements. "Give me a treat because I'm not doing something wrong. I deserve a reward because I've stopped some bad behavior."

There is a sense of cause and effect, action and reward. But you need to know that it is damaging to behave this way if you are trying to build trust. With your betrayal of the relationship, you forfeited any right to demand a reward for your newfound integrity and good behavior.

The second caveat is that you cannot expect your spouse to believe these things are sincere, genuine, or permanent. When you, by God's grace, shift your heart, mind, and actions toward winning your wife's heart back, she is going to be incredibly skeptical. Her veil of criticism and self-protection will cloud what appears to be your authentic change so that it is very difficult for her to consider you worthy of belief.

I compare this response of a wife to what the apostle Paul faced during and after his conversion as he interacted with people and attempted to integrate with other Christians. Ananias, the guy who was sent to meet Paul after his conversion, was terrified of this Pharisee who was a chief persecutor of Christians! And the Christians with whom Paul would become close and do ministry with were also initially afraid of him. And why not? Paul was an enemy of the early church. He was passionate about snuffing out the smoldering embers of Christianity:

> "Lord," Ananias answered, "I have heard many reports about this
> man and all the harm he has done to your saints in Jerusalem."
> (Acts 9:13)

Paul himself wrote,

> I too was convinced that I ought to do all that was possible to oppose
> the name of Jesus of Nazareth. (Acts 26:9)

> For you have heard of my previous way of life in Judaism, how
> intensely I persecuted the church of God and tried to destroy it.
> (Galatians 1:13)

But Paul had an intensely personal encounter with the living God that changed him radically, forever. In that experience, God changed his heart and mind, helping him see the misapplication of his fervor.

It is a strange story, though, in that he was a blind Pharisee named Saul for a few days before becoming the apostle known as Paul:

> Then Ananias went to the house and entered it. Placing his hands on
> Saul, he said, "Brother Saul, the Lord—Jesus, who appeared to you on
> the road as you were coming here—has sent me so that you may see
> again and be filled with the Holy Spirit." Immediately, something like
> scales fell from Saul's eyes, and he could see again. He got up and was
> baptized, and after taking some food, he regained his strength.

Saul spent several days with the disciples in Damascus. At once he began to preach in the synagogues that Jesus is the Son of God. All those who heard him were astonished and asked, "Isn't he the man who raised havoc in Jerusalem among those who call on this name? And hasn't he come here to take them as prisoners to the chief priests?" Yet Saul grew more and more powerful and baffled the Jews living in Damascus by proving that Jesus is the Christ. (Acts 9:17–22)

Later, Paul returned to Jerusalem to connect with the apostles. Here's how it went:

When he came to Jerusalem, he tried to join the disciples, but they were all *afraid* of him, not believing that he really was a disciple. (Acts 9:26, emphasis added)

So the guy God appointed to help with the conversion experience (Ananias) along with the disciples who were supposed to be kindred spirits were all afraid of him. It took a consistent change in his actions over time, and testimony from those who would vouch for him, to change the minds of his skeptics.

My point is this: because Paul had a track record of inflicting pain and persecution, the people in his life were cynical and critical of his change. And they had every right to be. They were hesitant to buy it. The process of gaining credibility and trust took the good apostle over three years! (See Galatians 1:18.)

Paul was living a new life in Arabia, and you would think word would have gotten back to the apostles that he was different. Surely they'd heard rumors that his heart and life were changed, that he was one of them. But upon meeting him, the disciples still held him at arm's length, reluctant to believe he had changed. After three *years*.

Such is the case with many wives. They just can't take their husband's change at face value. There has to be consistent change, over time, and even someone else to vouch for their husband's authenticity—which, by the way, is a great reason for men to have accountability partners. This becomes more important if you have a long track record of infidelity. The pain you've caused is deep, and the persecution you've committed is personal. The people in your life whom you most want to convince that you're different will likely be the most difficult to convince.

In the face of skepticism and doubt, it is still possible to build trust. With effort, energy, and divine guidance, these tools will help you build trust back into your relationship.

With that in mind, let's jump in.

## SPIRITUAL FERVENCY

Where are you with God right now? Who is he to you? How vibrant is your spiritual life? Have you used spirituality as a smokescreen to hide behind? Have you used it to manipulate your spouse? Was there a time when you felt more on fire, more passionate toward God?

In all likelihood, your spouse is asking these questions of you. She may even be asking these questions of herself. Whether outwardly or silently to herself, she is wondering about you and God. If your wife does not trust you but trusts God, and she sees you aligning yourself with him, her perception of your trustworthiness will begin to shift. If she does not trust you and also does not trust God, then the ante has gone up for you, and I'll explain this shortly.

For me, I needed something that characterized the first couple of years of my journey after my disclosure. I came up with "Nothing on the planet will stop me from becoming the man God is calling me to be." Whenever I repeated that phrase, it reminded me that the most important thing in my life was not my wife, Shelley, and not rebuilding trust, but passionately pursuing the character that God was trying to develop in me. A by-product of that pursuit was the restoration of trust and our relationship. Shelley knew that for me to be chasing the heart of God meant that I wouldn't be acting out sex-ually. The two cannot coexist.

If your energy is directed at serving, loving, engaging the sanctification process, worshiping, and deepening your relationship with God, there is no space to act out sexually. I'm not saying you'll fill up your time with church stuff. But I am saying that you'll fill up your heart with church stuff. When your wife sees your energy being channeled toward God, it places more Legos on the trust sculpture. She knows that if you're spending your energy there, you're not spending it elsewhere. She knows the man God is calling you to be won't stomp on her heart. She can be confident the character he wants to develop in you will serve her with humility and love rather than serve yourself with arrogance and entitlement.

Another very important thing happens when she sees you chasing the heart of God: it gives her a new lens through which to decipher your motives. It answers the question of why you are going to change. Are you trying to change yourself for her or allowing him to change you for him?

Can you see the difference? One will be temporary, the other permanent. Our wives certainly want us to change for them. But they don't want us to change for them alone. They want us to change for us and for God too. You need to realize that there is an incredible amount of pressure on a wife when she is your primary motivation for change. Wives know that this is a setup to be hurt again. They can be certain the day will come when they will let you down or disappoint you in some way. When that happens, the question is, will you choose to be faithful or will you choose to return to your old ways? Then they will feel like the cause of your sexual sin, and that's the last place a wife wants to be.

Try to see her perspective here. She doesn't want to give you any more justification to act out than you've already come up with on your own. To hear you say "You disappointed me, so I had a right to act out" is devastating.

She has to begin to believe that you are living for something greater than yourself, bigger than her, and more compelling than your marriage. Not your career, not your physical fitness, not sports, not your hobbies, not your ministry, not your finances, not your kids.

But God.

So think about those questions at the beginning of this section. Where are you with God? Who is he to you? Is he the distant creator God or the personal, loving father God? Are you connected or distant?

Maybe you have been hiding from him because you feel cut off and ashamed, and you're unwilling to be in his presence. Or maybe, like me, through the course of your struggles, you've prayed a bajillion times for him to show up, but he has been silent. You might be questioning if he is even real. That's okay. Start a new search.

A couple of books I recommend to reenergize your faith are *God\*Stories* by Andrew Wilson and *With* by Skye Jethani. These can be good places to start if the Bible doesn't seem to fit together or make much sense to you.

If you have hidden behind your spirituality or used it manipulatively, rebuilding trust is going to be more difficult, because you won't get as much trust-building mileage out of your spiritual fervency. You can understand why: your wife will think it's an instant replay of the painful past. The hiding usually takes the form of minimization. "I'm struggling with sin" was a cover for "I'm a serial adulterer and have been repeatedly stomping on your heart."

Another dodge that seems to come up often is a husband who says of his wife, "You're not the Holy Spirit, so it's not your place to judge my sin." Dude, give me a break! That's just a chintzy way of saying, "Stop demanding that I step up and be the kind of man and husband you deserve."

Another evasion is especially hurtful to a wife: "The Bible says we are not to withhold from one another, and that your body is not your own. So I think you should have more sex with me." As we said before, this is a cover for "I'm going to use the Bible to justify my selfish misuse of my sexuality and insist you be my prostitute." If these statements or similar ones ring a bell, you'll have to be intentional about sharing how your spiritual journey is leading you away from manipulation and hiding. You'll need to express how God is molding you into someone who applies the Word to himself rather than to other people for your own benefit.

Commit to deepening your spiritual walk. Commit to regularly reading the Bible and books that will help you understand God better. Commit to listening to podcasts from your favorite pastors. Commit to sharing what you are learning about yourself and God with your spouse.

I don't know of anything that has more power to rebuild trust than a wife seeing her husband passionately chase the heart of God.

## LEADING HER SPIRITUALLY

What does it mean to lead your wife spiritually? Most men I talk to can give me a biblically based answer, but they have a terribly difficult time expounding on how it looks in real life. It's not rocket science, but sometimes it sure feels like it. Rather than give you specific directions on how to lead your wife spiritually, I think it is more prudent to help you know how to have conversations about this topic.

Wives I counsel express many variations of how they want to be led spiritually. At one end of the continuum, some wives say they don't want anything spiritually from their lying/cheating/[insert derogatory term here] husband. They don't want to hear a word about God, Jesus, or anything related to Scripture. At the other end, wives tell me they are dying to be led. They long to hear their husband pray for them and their kids. They yearn to hear about a spiritual revelation or insight he has gained from his time in the Word. They desperately want him to initiate and lead them in a couples' devotional time several nights a week. Perhaps the needle is somewhere in between at your house.

My advice—assuming your personal spiritual fervency is in place—is to have regular conversations with your wife about what she needs or wants from you spiritually. Ask her if she'd be put off or offended if you share something from your devotional time. Inquire as to whether or not she wants to process the Sunday message from church as you drive to lunch. See if she's interested in doing a devotional together.

I recently talked about this with my friend Jim Phillis, another staff member at the Every Man's Battle Workshop. He says that a primary aspect of spiritual leadership in his home means being quick to admit wrongs and ask for forgiveness. Admitting wrongs is spiritual leadership? I never thought of it that way. Nor would I, had we not had this conversation.

Such may be the case with you and your wife. Your initiation of these conversations will be trust building in itself. The positive by-product is that you'll know what she expects and desires, which you can blend with your own ideas and creativity to get a sense of how to move forward.

I mentioned earlier that the ante goes up when your wife is struggling with trusting God. She may be in a tough place spiritually or even a nonbeliever. Consider for a minute what a testimony it would be for her to see you allow God to change you. How powerful for your wife to have a front-row seat to watch God at work in your life! The consistency and intentionality with which you pursue God may be the very thing that helps restore or even begins to develop your wife's faith.

INSIGHT FROM STEPHEN ARTERBURN

## Feed Your Faith

Throughout every phase of trust rebuilding, don't neglect to nurture your faith. Grow your faith in daily time alone with God. In addition to your recovery work, be involved in a Bible study or small group that nourishes and strengthens your faith. Scripture clearly points out how important endurance is in healing from our struggles.

The endurance process increases our character, something that may have been stagnant for many years. When you are a person of character, you have hope. Your faith in the midst of trials leads you to hope. Without faith or evidence that faith is placed in something worthy of our faith, we will lose hope. Hope sustains us and prevents us from self-annihilation. Without hope we self-destruct.

So grow stronger in your faith so that when you hit another unexpected bump in the road, you have hope that on the other side of it is something—someone—that makes it all worth it.

# 8

# Honesty

I'd rather lose you than lie to you." As a person who betrayed your wife's trust, this must be your mantra. A shift must occur in your paradigm of honesty that puts the truth in a place of utmost importance and highest priority. Chances are that more than one area of your life is permeated by a lack of honesty and integrity. But with this shift to prioritize honesty, every area of your life will be impacted by your relentless pursuit of the truth. And your wife must see this shift if trust is to be rebuilt between the two of you.

We tend to be a little fickle with honesty. What do you say when your wife asks, "Does this make me look fat?" or "How does this look on me?"

"Uh…um…you look…uh…it's kinda…well…"

Sound familiar? The last thing you want to do is hurt her feelings, so a little white lie is okay in this case, right? If so, then where is the line that separates little white lies from not so little lies anymore? Does Jesus make provisions for little lies? Is there room for skewing the truth? Even just a little? What do you think?

I'd say the answer is no.

If your target is building trust, and your commitment is steadfast to that end, then white lies are off the table. Period. In any situation. If your wife catches you in a white lie, she will likely extrapolate that to the whole of your life. She'll think that a little lie here equals big lies *there*.

If you'll lie about being a few minutes late to dinner, you'll probably lie about looking at porn again. If you can't tell the truth about what route you took home from work, then you probably won't tell the truth about contacting your mistress again. If you can't be honest about how much money you spent on a new tool, then it wouldn't be a stretch for you to lie about your whereabouts last Friday night.

Further, if you've been busted in your struggle or addiction, you probably lied about it in some form or fashion along the way. You lied about the severity of it or the intensity or the duration or the time line or maybe the people involved. The extrapolation your wife makes is justified.

Although it may frustrate you, try not to be offended if your wife expands something that seems like a minor omission or a nuance of the truth into something much larger. She is merely expressing her hurt, not attempting to indict you for a crime you did not commit. Realize that her pain is intense because you have committed other grave crimes. She's trying to communicate her pain to you.

"I'd rather lose you than lie to you" means that you plan to work with her in truth at all costs, even when it hurts. Even when you know it's not what she wants to hear. Even when the outcome doesn't make sense.

Here are a couple of examples of how this works in my house. Recently, Shelley was preparing for a speaking engagement and inviting my feedback on her wardrobe. She asked the ever daunting Catch-22 question "How does this look?"

Everything in me wanted to answer, "Great, looks great. You should wear that if it makes you comfortable." But that's not what I was thinking. I thought her outfit looked like something my grandmother would wear. The reality is that it would've been a lie to avoid the truth. At the very least it would have been an inauthentic response.

So I said, "That sweater looks kind of grandma-ish."

She bustled away, mumbling, "I don't know why I even ask you!"

I didn't know why she had asked me either if she didn't want the truth.

But I'd rather lose her than lie to her. So, to the best of my ability, I'll tell the truth in all things—and take my lumps.

Then there was the time Shelley asked me to ask our electrician a specific question. I talked to him later that day and asked him a bunch of my own questions but forgot to ask hers. When I returned home and she probed about her question, I hemmed and hawed and guessed the right answer based on my conversation with the electrician. She accepted my confusing response, but I could see it didn't sit well with her. And I knew in my gut I was lying. So I told her, "I forgot to ask." I had to call him to get an answer to her question.

Unfortunately, with her disappointment a likely result, it is sometimes easier to make something up and lie than tell the truth. And since we're dealing in truth, here's what I know to be truth in my life: if I start lying about small things, it's only a matter of time before I start lying about big things. That's dangerous. That's unsafe. That's untrustworthy.

This last example is a good segue into an area that needs to be addressed specifically when it comes to truth telling: withholding. If you withhold information, you lie. Let me say that a different way: when you choose not to disclose pertinent information, you aren't telling the truth.

Some people will try to dance around this and manipulate a situation for their protection and benefit. They'll convince themselves that not sharing information means not lying about it. "If I don't tell her about it, then I'm not lying about it." Wrong! And untruthful. If there is *material information* (a technical term used during my days as an accountant and consultant) related to a situation, and you decide not to disclose it, you're guilty of misleading your client. What is material? Pretty much everything.

For example, let's say that you struggle with Internet pornography. You've accessed it at work a few times, but you do this mostly at home. Your wife busts you, then demands to know how big this issue is. You tell her about every instance you can remember of accessing porn at home—but withhold the part about doing it at work. You've just lied. Whether you accidentally left that part out or not, in her eyes, you just lied. And trust is further from being rebuilt.

Perhaps we should define *material* as any information that if left undisclosed now but discovered later would cause pain, discouragement, and distrust in your spouse. Does that cover it? If you're like I was in the beginning of my restoration with Shelley, you understand this new definition of lying to be way broader than any you would have chosen yourself.

Another thing you need to know about honesty is just how big the impact of lying is. I cannot tell you how many wives have relayed to me their disappointment and discouragement with lying. It's even bigger than acting out. Wives will often say they can forgive and get past the acting out again, but they really struggle with and often cannot get past the lies and secrets. In fact, I have talked to very few wives who say they would absolutely divorce over another slip or relapse of sexual integrity. They can somehow muster the grace to move past it, assuming their husband is genuinely working on making things better. Alternatively, they repeatedly say that they will not tolerate another lie. Period. End of story.

*If you are to build trust and win your wife back, you cannot afford to lie.*

In a recent counseling session, a wife discovered that her husband had contacted a former girlfriend on Facebook. He had disclosed multiple affairs to his wife, many of which began on Facebook. (I'll address social media a little later.) The wife knew he was doing it again.

When she confronted him, he lied and she dropped the hammer. She told me she would have worked with him to take the necessary steps to reconcile after another affair, but because of his lying, she was done. She filed divorce papers a few weeks later.

You might lose your wife by telling her the truth, but at least there is a chance to salvage the relationship. What I mean is that your wife may ultimately choose to leave based on how you have wronged her and violated your marriage vows. You cannot control that. It is her choice. Alternatively, you put the final nails into your own coffin when you lie.

*I'd rather lose you than lie to you.*

## Active Truth Telling

This concept is certainly nothing new or novel, but it requires clarification for many men. *Passive truth telling* means there is a willingness to be honest about something when specific questions are asked. *Active truth telling* means being honest before being questioned. Taking it a step further, it means anticipating questions that might be asked and answering them ahead of time.

At this point, a lot of guys will say, "You want me to be a mind reader?"

No, that is not what I am suggesting. What I am proposing is that you treat your wife like a partner, not a baby-sitter. As a colaborer in the business of life rather than a parent. It is important to get out of your self-centered way of thinking and walk a few steps in your spouse's shoes. Take a few minutes to consider what she might need to know, might be anxious about, might doubt you on, or perhaps what she could be fearful of.

Your wife needs access to all bank and credit card accounts so she can see what is happening at any given time. (This will be covered more thoroughly in chapter 18.) Open access is a good thing, and a husband who is willing to grant access to all his accounts demonstrates transparency. However, this is still a passive form of truth telling. He is passively allowing his wife to check up on him when she wants to. He doesn't have to do anything but wait. She has to be the active participant.

Too many wives tell me they feel like they are thrust into a private investigator role and must dig to find the truth. Or worse, they feel as though they are baby-sitters, having to make sure the child they care for hasn't left behind a mess for them to clean up. Active truth telling relieves them of this burden.

When a husband becomes an active participant or active truth teller, he relieves his wife of the responsibility of checking up on him. Being an active truth teller means not only granting access to the accounts but also proactively initiating the review of the accounts. He would suggest he download the week's transactions on Friday afternoon and sit down with his wife that night and explain each item line by line if she wants him to.

The conversation might sound like this: "Honey, I want to build trust with you in the area of our finances. I don't want you to feel like a baby-sitter or a private investigator. And I don't want you to feel like there is something not clear about our finances and how I'm spending our money. To that end, here are the usernames and passwords to all of our and my accounts. (Give her a piece of paper with everything written out.) Further, I'd like to sit down with you at the end of each week and go over them line by line and explain what they are. If you have any questions, you can ask me. Once we're done, you can rest knowing that each week's spending is in the light. So on Friday, when I get home from work, I'll download and print out each record for the week. Anything I can't explain immediately, I'll research and get back to you within twenty-four hours. Would you be willing to do this with me?"

The objective is not to painstakingly detail your every movement and dollar spent (although that might be a by-product of this exercise), but rather to proactively live your life in the light, taking responsibility for righting any wrongs and displaying a contrite initiative that speaks louder than your past actions.

Here's another example of active versus passive truth telling. Say a man's issue has been accessing Internet pornography after his wife has gone to bed. What would be passive and what would be active truth telling? Passive truth telling might look like slapping X3watch on your laptop and calling it good. If there is an issue, she'll know and say something. Then you can explain it.

Hopefully there won't be an issue, right? Wrong. There will be. And a Lego or two of trust will be destroyed.

Active truth telling in this case has a couple of components. First, if you've installed an Internet filter and monitoring software, you need to know that they are imperfect. There will be false positives and negatives. Some things will show up on a report that look like integrity violations but actually aren't, and some things that look sketchy in your Internet history will be left out of the report. It's the nature of the beast.

You can actively tell the truth by beating the report at reporting your activities. Much like the money example above, proactively reviewing Internet travels and history prior to receiving a monitoring report would be very helpful.

As a side note, do you know how much anxiety some wives experience before they receive the accountability report? There can be anticipatory anxiety, waiting for that day every week or two when the accountability report comes, that is so strong it can be debilitating. Some wives dread waiting for the next time they find out their husband cheated on them—again.

That's what it feels like. Getting her heart stomped on over and over.

Active truth telling includes identifying patterns of acting-out behavior and communicating about corrective behaviors. In this case, the acting out occurs late at night, after the wife has gone to bed—this is the pattern.

Correcting that could include a boundary of not being online after your spouse has turned in or simply going to bed at the same time. In either event, the anomaly can be proactively explained—and possibly even preempted—so as to ease your wife's mind.

Again, she shouldn't have to ask, "What did you do after I went to bed?" Instead, a proactive truth teller would initiate the conversation with something like, "I just want you to know what I did last night after you went to bed. I don't want you to have to ask about it or be nervous about it. I closed my computer at 9:15 after having finished my document for work today. Here's the laptop with my history pulled up so you can verify. From 9:15 to 10:00 I watched the rest of *The Office.* From 10 to 10:15 I watched the news on channel 7. From 10:15 to 10:30 I shaved, brushed, flossed, used the bathroom, then hopped in bed."

Can you see the parts of the conversation that are meaningful? There are details, clarity, and very little room for discrepancy. When you beat your wife to the punch, preempting her questions, you build trust. That doesn't mean she won't have some questions of her own based on what you've shared. That's fine, because it's intimacy then.

The important point is that you spoke up to put her mind at ease. There is so much mileage to be gained in active truth telling. It relieves a wife of any need to investigate or interrogate. It can be a tangible change she sees in you that she can objectively say is different. That builds trust.

## BLACK AND WHITE

You can no longer live in any gray areas where there's room to misinterpret any of your actions or words. It is worth mentioning here that there's a distinct difference in the preciseness of recollection between wives and husbands. Many detail-oriented wives are married to generality-driven husbands. As it pertains to trust building, preciseness is critical.

For example, if the current time is 1:43 p.m. and your wife asks you what time it is, what would you say? Would you say the time is a quarter of two, two-ish, about two o'clock, or about twenty till two? If so, you're dealing in gray areas. You might be perceived as not telling the truth. When it's generalities versus details, preciseness must prevail. The time is 1:43 p.m.!

If you spent $7.59 on your lunch, and your wife asks how much it cost, how would you respond? Eight bucks? Seven fifty?

*Gray area. Potential lie.*

Now you may push back on this and say that kind of exactness is a little over the top, but if you're trying to build trust, you can't afford to be anything other than over the top. Maybe your wife isn't that detail oriented, so you think that being exact to the penny or minute wouldn't be that meaningful for her. To the contrary, I can assure you that the effort you put into being that precise will certainly be noticed.

Every place you can do something to communicate your intention, your commitment, and your heart for honesty will be another Lego placed on the sculpture of your restored relationship.

There are many reasons men deal in gray areas. For some, it involves a fear of failure. In a simple but powerful way, there is a sense of failure in saying you'll be home in fifteen minutes but it ends up taking seventeen minutes. Some men just don't want to be wrong, especially if a wife's hopes or expectations are hanging on him being right.

Other men who dabble in gray areas are responding to feelings of impotence and being controlled. They view their wife's questions about details as an interrogation and an attempt to control their every move. The truth is, it may be just that! But now is not the time to react and rebel against it, and you don't have a leg to stand on if you've violated her trust.

Let me reiterate the point: deal in the details, because they're the currency of trust building. Your willingness to get specific, be detail oriented, and work in black and white fosters an environment where trust can thrive.

INSIGHT FROM STEPHEN ARTERBURN

## Watch Out for Overconfidence

There are several missteps you can make in recovery, and the biggest one is getting to that point where you think you have it made—you are beyond the basic practices that brought you hope and progress in the first place. I am sure you are familiar with people with bipolar disorder who need medication to function normally. They take the medication and feel so much better that they start to think they no longer need the medication. Rather than being glad the medication has allowed them to experience an amazing turn-around, they want to turn their backs on it. The result is predictable. They revert back to their old patterns and behaviors until they get so bad they are convinced that medication is not optional. Do yourself a favor and view your recovery in that same way.

In addition to not convincing yourself that you are strong enough to get better on your own, don't convince yourself that you don't now or never will need additional counseling. In other words, as helpful as this book can be, you may need some additional help.

Rather than trying to eliminate things, look at what you can do to secure and strengthen your progress. All of us need additional wisdom from others, which may include formal counseling. Don't be shocked if you find that from time to time you are in need of addi-tional help to fix some things or to grow deeper and stronger in your recovery.

If your wife knows that you will get help on your own when you sense you need it, she will trust you even more! Some people even come back through the Every Man's Battle Workshop again. Better to do it to prevent a relapse than to do it after a relapse—and have your wife's trust shattered again.

Stay on top of your temptations and be ready to respond with actions rather than complacency.

# 9

# Transparency in the Big and Little Things

B y now I hope you understand that building trust requires total honesty. There can be no more lies, secrets, vague responses, or defensiveness. There can be nothing hidden, and your wife must have access to everything. While this may be overkill, I really want you to get this! I want you to firmly grasp every nuance of trust building, which is why I'm including this chapter on transparency.

First, you have to be able to distinguish between transparency and translucency. Transparency does not diffuse light; thus, what is beyond can be seen clearly. However, translucency diffuses light so that what is beyond is not clear. You know how frustrating it can be to look at something through a translucent window? You can see something is happening on the other side, but you can't make out exactly what. You see shadows and occasional distinguishing features, but the picture is never clear.

So you start making up scenarios in your head. Maybe it's not a tree limb brushing against the window but a burglar trying to break in. Maybe it's a positive conversation and the coworker in the boss's office is getting a promotion and a raise. Maybe your colleague is getting laid off—and it's your turn next.

Translucency leaves details to your imagination, and in the case of a relationship damaged by sexual integrity issues, this is going to end badly. If there is doubt, there must be deceit, or so goes the thinking in the mind of a wife whose heart has been violated.

It's the difference between true and mostly true, between total honesty and partial honesty. If you are trying to win back your wife and rebuild trust, you cannot afford to have any translucent glass in your life. Your windows must be completely transparent to your wife. If you have nothing to hide, the only difficulty you'll have with this will be the fact that you simply haven't lived this way in the past. But now you're developing a new way of life. Your standard for living aboveboard is changing. And it will take time for her to really *know* this.

This section dovetails with the previous discussions about details and gray areas. When you operate translucently, your wife usually feels compelled to be a detective. A wife knows when she's not getting the full story, even if she cannot put her finger on exactly what's amiss. Wives have a sixth sense about these things; they know when something is wrong.

I have heard too many wives say they feel like a private investigator when they talk with their husband about topics like sexual integrity. They feel like they have to ask the right question in just the right way in order to get the full answer. In other words, they can see something behind their husband's translucence, but they're not sure just what it is.

My dad used to tell me that when you assume, you make an ass out of you and me. Likewise, when we leave it up to our wife to assume what we have or haven't done, we only make an ass out of ourselves. We break down trust rather than build it up. When we are reluctant to share any details and we choose our words carefully, we lose transparency. Our behavior becomes clouded. When you stop micromanaging the details and tell the whole truth—even when it hurts—then you're free to be transparent.

This strikes at the heart of a regular complaint of husbands: "My wife asks too many questions. She nags and nags, like an interrogator." Typically a wife does this because she doesn't believe you're telling the whole truth.

You're coming across to her as translucent. She may ask the same question many times even when you are transparent—we've discussed the reasons for this and the need for you to patiently allow it.

Wives ask questions because they are continually seeking reassurance, but their questioning is different from what we perceive as an interrogation. When a wife drills with pointed questions and asks for specifics, it's because she doesn't believe she's getting adequate or pertinent information. Here's a sample.

WIFE: How many times have you looked at porn this year?

HUSBAND: I don't know, maybe twelve times.

WIFE: *Every month?* When every month?

HUSBAND: I don't recall when every month. About once a month.

WIFE: While I was at work? While *you* were at work? When I was taking the kids to school? The week of our anniversary? *When?*

HUSBAND: Not the week of our anniversary.

WIFE: I can't believe you. When I was at the family reunion in June, did you then?

HUSBAND: I don't remember. That was five months ago. It might have been during that time, yes.

WIFE: Ah! You waited until I was out of town. When? The first night I was gone? After we hung up the phone that night?

HUSBAND: I don't remember what time it was! Is it really that important what time I looked at porn?

You get the drift. This dialogue is a common one in my office. The questions start out as general, perhaps in large time frames (for example, "last year"). Then, when the husband's response is curt, translucent, vaguely honest but inconclusive, the questions become more and more specific and detailed (for example, down to the specific hour).

The last question the husband asks in the example is not out of the ordinary either: "Is it really that important what time I looked at porn?" Well, the reality is it might not have been that important if he had been transparent at the outset of the conversation.

The more it appears a husband is withholding information, the more likely a wife will take on the interrogator role. And much like a detective trying to solve a murder, every detail becomes important. Just as it is for a character in a movie, the more personal the horrific event and the more mystery surrounding it, the more intensely committed the investigator becomes to solving the crime.

Here is an example of how that conversation could go. What you need to know is that it may not skip the interrogation, but transparency will give you a better chance to avoid one. Obviously, if you've spent many years being translucent, then a single transparent conversation will not convince your spouse that things have really changed.

WIFE: How many times have you looked at porn this year?
HUSBAND: Honey, I have looked at porn every month this year. To the best of my recollection, I looked one time each month. I remember January, on about the fourteenth. I remember because that's how long I kept my new year's resolution to not look. I don't remember when in February, March, or April. I do remember May though; it was unfortunately the week of our anniversary. I'm sorry for that. I remember June, too. It was the day after you got back from the family reunion. I don't remember July, August, or September. Well, maybe September; it might have been Labor Day. Last month, October, it was the night before Halloween. This month I haven't looked at porn. Most often I have done it late at night, either after you've gone to bed or I would get up in the middle of the night. I accessed porn on my laptop, using an alternate username so you

wouldn't find it. The username is ————. I would usually spend a
half hour. There were a couple of times, two, I think, where I spent
only ten minutes. And there were two times where I spent an hour.
Usually it's about thirty minutes.

WIFE: *Every month?*

HUSBAND: Every month. I'm sorry. I'm open to answering any question
you have where I left things unclear.

You see the difference. What I am suggesting is that transparency means
you offer as many details and circumstances as you can think of. Try to an-
ticipate what your wife might want to know. You don't need to be a mind
reader. But you can be accommodating, proactive, and empathetic enough to
help her avoid taking on a private investigator role.

Remember, most wives don't want to be in that role and are incredibly
disappointed in themselves when they adopt it. That in turn just makes them
more angry with their husband, whom they believe forced them to take on
the role in the first place. You can end the cycle by being transparent.

## DETAILS

Unfortunately, anything that can look suspicious will look suspicious. This is
true as it pertains to the details of life. If you are like me, and details are not
your thing—you think high level and in generalities—it's going to take intentionality on your part to change.

Most wives are detail oriented. They remember dates, names, numbers,
colors, places, people, and other facts about most of the situations they've
encountered. They remember what clothes they wore on their honeymoon,
what was served for dinner at a wedding you attended fifteen years ago, the
name of your coworker from the job you had during college, and the full
sixteen-digit number from the credit card you canceled ten years ago.

And then there are men. We can hardly remember what we had for dinner last night. We don't remember many details, especially not the things we're incredibly ashamed of. There is, however, one caveat: sports. We can remember all the stats of our favorite players and games. Yet we can't recollect the details of our acting-out behavior.

You need to shift your energies. You need to craft your skill with details toward your wife and your life rather than your favorite running back. It never ceases to amaze me that some men know how many sacks their favorite defensive end had last year, yet they struggle to remember their anniversary and certainly can't recall their wife's shoe size.

Warning: If you want to grow trust, it is imperative to reorient yourself to recognize the details of life and relationships. As this pertains to the disclosure process, I encourage you to let your wife be the judge of how much she wants to know. She also can decide how little information she needs in terms of details or how exacting your information must be to satisfy her need for the truth.

Often men will say they don't want to share the details of their indiscretions because it will hurt their wife. If that's your case, let me suggest that you abdicated your protective right by acting out and choosing to violate her trust. You could have protected your wife by not acting out in the first place. Wives often react strongly to this hypocrisy. If you are trying to protect her by not sharing the details of your behavior, that can easily be confused with hiding information and thus looking as if you aren't serious about changing and healing.

As I write this, Shelley and I are about a decade into the process of healing, and we still deal with things that trigger her distrust, such as details that remind her of my hurtful past behavior. I'm a fan of wives asking questions and getting the information they need. I'm not a fan of their getting all the information they want just because they want it.

If you are a wife reading this, I urge you to ask yourself twice if you really need the information you are asking for. These details will often be etched in your mind, and some, unfortunately, will not go away.

If you're a husband reading this, it isn't your job to decide what your wife needs to know. It is the wife's responsibility to decide how much she wants to know.

## Shelley's Thoughts

Indeed, it is different for every wife as to how much detail she wants. For me, I needed to know the details in order to know what I needed to forgive Jason for. I tried the no-details route at first, but it came back to bite me when I realized how bitter and resentful my heart was toward Jason about things I didn't even really know! Not only did I want to know the details in order to forgive him, but I wanted to know so there wouldn't be any secrets between us like there had been during all of our relationship to that point. It's risky to know it all, but for me it was worth it.

That being said, I reached a point in our process when I realized ruminating over the details and asking questions about the details would never quench my thirst to know. I realized I'd never be able to completely make sense of my husband's actions. So while knowing the details was important, my knowing created another challenge: subconsciously thinking that knowing the details would heal me. Thus, I had to work on not allowing my drive to understand everything through the details hinder my healing process on the road to forgiveness and wholeness.

Take Away: Remember that this is your wife's journey too, and bringing your darkest secrets into the light can be the framework for rebuilding connection and emotional intimacy with her.

I want to explain one more thing about details and trust building. When husbands are vague and do not deal in the details, many wives conjure up suspicions far more terrible than the truth. If your wife is hurt because you've violated trust in a deep way, your lack of details opens the door for her to think the worst. Rather than give you the benefit of any doubt, she may fill in the blanks with the most hurtful assumptions. Her logic says that if you aren't willing to share the details, then the truth must be very bad. If it weren't that bad, you would simply tell her about it.

If you want to rebuild trust, you cannot afford to have her thinking the worst.

## INSIGHT FROM STEPHEN ARTERBURN

### Confession

The most specific direction on healing in the Bible comes from James 5:16, where we are told to confess our sins to each other and pray for each other if we want to experience healing. What a sense of relief we have when we move beyond our secret shame and open up to each other in humble confession. When you confess to your wife, it may produce initial pain and struggle, but it will lead to a deeper and richer healing for her and your relationship.

Our basic tendency is to cover up and preserve an appearance of being above temptation and certainly above sin. Confession humbles us to a reality where we don't know what tomorrow may bring and whether we will be strong enough to handle it well. So we bring alongside what is necessary to succeed. We utilize the resources of support, encouragement, and accountability to stay the course and succeed in our mission toward greater integrity and restored trust in our marriage.

# 10

# True Intimacy

What comes to mind when you read or hear the word *intimacy*? Do you think of sex? Do you think of closeness? Do you think of vulnerability?

Unfortunately, our supersexualized culture has degraded and narrowly focused the word *intimacy* to mean sex. We hear it in our speech. "They were intimate" means they had sex. We see it in marketing, meaning clothes worn (albeit briefly) during sexual activity. But truly, there may be very little that is intimate about any of this.

If we are to rebuild trust in our damaged relationship with our wife, it is imperative to broaden our understanding of intimacy as well as the implications for relational closeness. Here's what Webster's says *intimacy* means: "something of a personal or private nature."

Hmm, that doesn't say sex, yet sex is intensely personal and private in nature. The dictionary definition doesn't say anything about closeness, yet relational closeness has the connotation of something personal in nature. Webster's doesn't distinctly mention vulnerability, yet vulnerability is inherently characteristic in letting someone else into the personal and private things in our life. Here's how I'd like to define intimacy for a person trying to rebuild trust with his wife:

A state of honesty, openness, vulnerability, transparency, and authenticity with oneself, God, and/or another person.

At the Every Man's Battle Workshop we say "into-me-see." If I had a vanity license plate, it might read N2MEC. If we're going to be intimate, we're going to allow someone to know our hopes, dreams, fears, desires, insecurities, thoughts, expectations, disappointments, prayers, and more. Can two people have sex without any of these things being communicated? Well, yes. In fact, many people reveal that there is no intimacy by their sexual integrity issues.

True intimacy is characterized by a depth of knowing that includes facts and figures and also transcends these things and moves toward the other person's soul. The benefits of true intimacy include feeling loved, accepted, warmed, comforted, forgiven, connected, desired, safe, and secure.

However, true intimacy requires a huge risk—the possibility of rejection. What if we allow someone to see into us, and they don't like what they see? What if they decide they don't respect us or want to be around us because of who we are? Ouch!

Sexual temptation is sometimes referred to as false intimacy because it appears to offer all the benefits of intimacy without requiring any risk to the recipients. Briefly and fraudulently you get to feel loved, warmed, desired, and accepted without having to risk being rejected.

So how does this relate to trust building? To begin with, intimacy is usually severely lacking when one person has sexual integrity issues. Certainly a false, fraudulent intimacy exists, but for such a man, in the most meaningful relationship in his life, intimacy is a notion, not a reality. For a wife to trust her husband, she must start to believe he is "letting her in." That is, she has to feel as though she knows him in a deeper, broader way, and with a sense of authenticity.

I often hear a spouse say of the other, "I don't even know this person. I've been fooled into thinking he/she is one way, when in fact he/she is someone completely different."

My wife will tell you that when she talked to my mistress and found out the truth of what was going on with me, it scared her. In a very deep way she had to acknowledge to herself that she had no clue who I was. She was, in fact, married to a stranger. I'll never forget coming home that night and hearing Shelley tell me I was an alien to her.

In order to establish trust, your wife has to begin to believe she's getting to know the real you. All of you. Your ins and outs. Your ups and downs. Not just your hypothesizing and pontificating, but your true feelings, thoughts, motives, and core values. You're going to be analyzed from the ground up and inside out.

I think a wife is innately endowed with a yearning to know the heart, mind, body, soul, and strength of her husband. In other words, just as we long for the living God to reveal himself to us, and we desire to press in to the mystery of who he is, so a wife longs for her husband to reveal himself so that she can trust him.

### Shelley's Thoughts

Jason and I were averse to intimacy while we were dating and during the first several years of our marriage—prior to my demand for full disclosure. We both had things we were holding closer to our heart than each other.

I had an eating disorder, and Jason had a sexual addiction. We were good for each other in that way, but it was terribly dysfunctional.

Going through the first couple of years of our healing process really helped us learn to become more intimate with each other, but it wasn't until I became involved in a support group for women dealing with their husband's betrayal that I really learned to be intimate and vulnerable with others. This has carried over into my relationship with Jason and has helped me to be truly intimate with him.

Take Away: I encourage you to consider joining a healthy support group with solid boundaries where you can begin to learn to be intimate with others. In addition, I challenge you to model the way your wife can learn to become more intimate with you!

It is important to note that intimacy has multiple components and types. Below is a list of the types of intimacy I try to be cognizant of at my house. It is interesting to see how these ebb and flow.

- **Intellectual Intimacy**: what we think about and how we cognitively process that information.
- **Emotional Intimacy**: how we feel and what/who we feel for.
- **Spiritual Intimacy**: our relationship with God. What he is showing and teaching us through life, our pastors, and our time in Scripture and prayer.
- **Recreational Intimacy**: how we have fun together.
- **Professional Intimacy**: how we engage and process our professional lives, whether this entails a career as a parent or as a corporate professional.
- **Proximal Intimacy**: physical closeness; for example, sitting next to each other on the couch.
- **Physical Intimacy (excluding sex)**: physical touching; for example, holding hands, hugs, massages, foot rubs.
- **Physical Intimacy (sex)**: sexual intimacy.

Sometimes when I'm working on intimacy issues with a couple, I'll ask them to identify when they recently initiated intimacy, which type, and when they reciprocated after their spouse initiated. Almost like clockwork, a couple experiencing a lack of trust will identify that very few, if any, of these types were initiated. Alternatively, a couple that is experiencing tentative yet hopeful moments of trust will be aware of and have engaged in several of these.

When building trust in your relationship, you need to be conscious of the types of intimacy and make a concerted effort to initiate them. Spiritual, emotional, and intellectual intimacy are of paramount importance early in the process. The other types come after these three. This is because the way you connect deeply with your spouse is by communicating your thoughts and emotions. When your wife believes she is seeing your true thought life and your honest emotions, she will feel closer and more connected to you. Later, the importance of emotional and intellectual intimacy doesn't diminish, and the other types grow in their own importance.

While you should initiate these types of intimacy, your wife will be the barometer of how strongly you should pursue them. Some types of intimacy—especially the last one, sexual physical intimacy—might be questionable, depending on where you are in the restoration process. At the moment, your spouse may not be ready, willing, or even remotely interested in sexual intimacy. So you should proceed cautiously and with open communication on this and any other forms of intimacy.

Men often ask how they can learn to do this. It's not rocket science. You simply talk about it. You say, "Honey, I'd like to be intimate with you. Do you mind if I sit next to you on the couch?" "Do you mind if we hold hands on this car ride?" "Can we talk about how your day with the kids went?" The point is this: go slow and be a gentle, intentional initiator.

Intimacy should not be a manipulation for sex. But some men (and women) use the different types of intimacy to do just that. It's as if the goal in life is to have sex. They'll sit and talk with their spouse, secretly (and sometimes not so secretly) hoping it will result in sex. One person will give the other a foot rub, hoping it leads to sex. You get the picture.

I can tell you that if you use the types of intimacy only to have sex, it will backfire. You'll corrupt each type and taint it with your motives. Your wife will have an increasingly difficult time trusting you, because it will be unclear who you are being intimate for—her or yourself.

Self-serving intimacy is not intimacy at all. It is manipulation.

Intimacy in the context of a relationship and by our definition is an engagement with another for the sake of deeper connection. It's not for the sake of sex.

Imagine that the person you're spending the rest of your life with is suddenly unable to be sexually intimate. Period. Never again. Will your relationship be shallow and disconnected? Will you be bitter and resentful? Or will you do everything you can to connect deeply without sex?

If you will pursue that kind of connection without sex now, while it is possible to have sex, you will see trust develop and your relationship grow.

Sex simultaneously delivers intimacy and is a product of intimacy. It should not be an end in itself. If you believe intimacy is solely about sex, please talk with your pastor or a counselor. This belief will keep you perpetually locked into a harmful dynamic, the hallmark of which is manipulating your spouse for sexual gratification.

## INSIGHT FROM STEPHEN ARTERBURN

### Feeling Truly Loved

This entire book is about rebuilding and strengthening the connection between your wife and you. The more trust there is, the deeper the connection will grow. And with that connection will come an experience that is extremely rare—the experience of being and feeling truly loved.

One of the horrible things about our lust addiction is that in whatever form it manifests, it creates a barrier between us and God, our wife, and everybody else. Feeling love from God once again and feeling it from others will enable you to provide love at a deeper level to your wife. Connection that is true and real will provide you with the love all of us flourish in when we experience it.

# 11

# Accountability

Building trust requires that you have others to whom you are accountable and who will vouch for you. In fact, accountability is important regardless of whether or not you are building trust. I don't believe you can find the healing you are looking for outside of having a group of men who are faithfully walking the journey with you. So how can accountability help restore trust? There are two answers to this question.

First, being accountable with a few safe, healthy men who are striving to be who God is calling them to be can only help you move in that same direction. When I was a teenager, my dad used to quote the familiar saying, "Birds of a feather flock together."

For a wife there is something special about knowing that honorable men surround her husband. If she knows you are required to give an account of your life on a weekly basis, she can relax a bit. She can relinquish a little control if she believes she is not the only one asking you what's going on in your mind, heart, and behavior. If she knows these men and respects them, she can rest a little easier that on multiple fronts you are being held to a higher standard.

Second, accountability can help build trust if your wife decides to call one of your accountability partners. If there is a man she respects who can vouch for you, it will go a long way toward her trusting you again. This can accomplish the same boost in credibility that Barnabas accomplished for Paul with the other disciples.

Earlier we saw that the disciples were skeptical about Paul when he returned to Jerusalem from Damascus. However, Barnabas vouched for him and helped convince them that he belonged and was trustworthy (see Acts 9:27). Your accountability partners can serve a similar purpose.

Many men push back on this point. They insist that accountability should be private and confidential and that a wife has no right to infringe on their freedom. In my experience, the guys who say that usually have something to hide. Seriously.

A man who sits in my office and is open, transparent, and honest and has fully disclosed his shortcomings to his wife typically says very little in his accountability group that his wife doesn't already know. For her to call one of his accountability partners and ask about his integrity will only strengthen his position and add Legos to the trust sculpture because she will find confirmation and reassurance of his journey.

I actually didn't know my wife called my accountability partners until several years into the process. First, they never told me she had called them. And second, she never said anything about it to me at the time. When I found out, I was encouraged and thankful because I knew my friends would affirm my character development and reassure Shelley that I was worth sticking around for.

If you feel a strong pushback to the idea that your wife could call any of your accountability partners at any time and ask for a report of your progress, you should challenge yourself. What do you have to hide? Why do you think you're entitled to confidentiality?

Don't lie to your accountability partners. Man up! If you fail, repent, ask for forgiveness, and move on.

## Effective Accountability

I'm often asked how accountability should work. While there is no magic formula, there are a few constants that should be present in any good accountability structure. Since this book is something of a field manual, I want to lay out in detail how I believe accountability should look to foster maximum growth and trust building.

## Who

To begin, let's define who should be an accountability partner. I am a fan of having multiple accountability partners, ideally three other guys. There are several reasons for this. One, you are almost guaranteed you will have at least one man to connect with when you show up for your accountability meeting. Every week somebody will have an appointment, will be sick or have sick kids, may have to travel for work, or might hit snooze too many times. When you walk in the door for your accountability meeting, you want to be certain someone will be there. It's not a good idea to miss a week for any reason! If everyone shows up, that's awesome! If not, *someone* will be there for you. This is important not only because it ensures you have someone to download with but also because it adds relational stability and a sense of security that offsets the temptation to sexually act out. One of the subtle but key hooks of sexually acting out is that it is always there for you. Porn is always available and ever present. Mistresses are always open to your advances. There is "security" in knowing your drug is always accessible. Hence you must offset this hook when you're in recovery by having your accountability partners reliably there for you.

So who should these three men be? This part is subjective. It is incredibly difficult to put parameters around the people you invite into your journey, but it's important to do so. For example, if one of your accountability partners espouses a womanizing lifestyle, hello!—he isn't going to give you wise counsel on how to honor your wife's anger, disappointment, and boundaries. He will detract from your trust-building efforts and, more important, from your character development. In this season of change, you cannot afford a setback.

The men you want walking with you should be men whose lives you would like to emulate. Ideally, they would also love Jesus and want to follow his ways. Sadly, in some instances, a non-Christian is less judgmental and more supportive. So if you have a good friend who is not a believer but is super supportive of you and your marriage, then invite him. But you want these guys to be pro-marriage, not just pro-you. If any of them have a "grass is always greener on the other side" attitude about their wife, they are not a good fit for your accountability group. You want guys who are trying humbly to love their wives as Christ loved the church.

Frankly, it ticks me off when a man violates his wife's heart through sexually acting out, be it adultery or pornography or raging lust, and then decides he's going to file for divorce. It's like throwing a grenade at your wife and then joining the enemy. The justification is typically shrouded in a bunch of accusations about how bad the past has been, how controlling the wife has been, how unhappy he has been for many years, blah blah blah. Really? Perhaps if you weren't acting out sexually and actually lived with integrity, as God requires, you would have been able to lead with humble servanthood and right the ship of your marriage. Instead, you took the lame, easy road to self-soothe and self-medicate, and now you're being a coward by not facing the damage you've caused.

Get in the ring and grapple with getting untangled from the barbed wire of your ego! Or go ahead and file for divorce—and live with the reality that when it came to the biggest fight of your life, you bowed out and threw in the towel. I'm not saying this to belittle you; I'm saying it to challenge you. I almost threw in the towel about nine months after disclosure. Thank the Lord my accountability partners wouldn't let me.

Back to your accountability group, you're looking for men who are at least as mature as you in their spiritual walk and maybe a few steps ahead of you. Some guys will ask their pastor to fill this role, and while that can work, I wouldn't advise it. Pastors have several people like you to walk the journey with, and they really can't be intimately involved in everyone's life. And many pastors won't or don't feel comfortable going into the deep, uncomfortable places you need to go for effective accountability. Vice versa, I hear guys say they don't want to know the nitty-gritty on their pastor; they would rather keep them on a pedestal as a spiritual hero.

For similar reasons, I am not a proponent of having family members as accountability partners. A brother might be okay, but certainly not a brother-in-law. It can be a difficult corner for a brother-in-law to be there for you when you disclose your junk, knowing it's going to directly affect his sister. *Awkward!*

Parents and fathers-in-law are out too for much the same reason. Do you really want to get gut-level honest with a father whose blood runs hot for protecting his sweet little girl? Frankly, none of your accountability partners should have a family connection with either you or your wife. I know you may have an extraordinary relationship with your father or father-in-law, but I've seen accountability arrangements detract from that relationship. If your father is your life mentor, a professional consultant to you, and a giant in the faith, keep it that way. If you want to invite him in and keep him updated on your progress, that's fantastic. But keep him on the periphery, not in your inner circle.

To whittle down the list even more, you want guys who are a few steps ahead of you on the recovery journey, or at the least aren't in the middle of blowing up their life like you have. That is not to say your partners haven't struggled, but you don't want the blind leading the blind. You want guys who can help pull you out of the pit with encouragement, insight, wisdom, guidance, suggestions, tools, tips, and tactics. While you're struggling, you don't want to have to pull them out of their own pits. They're going to have problems of their own. We all do. But they need to be working through their problems and heading toward health while at the same time showing you the way.

Does it sound difficult to find the right three men? It is. But remember, God is for you. He knows you need to be surrounded by great men. He knows you need to submit yourself to their authority and be led. I suspect he has already begun to orchestrate the connections you need. Let me explain how this worked for me.

In college, my friend James led the Campus Crusade for Christ men's group. I looked up to him and enjoyed our friendship. We clicked in many ways. After college we lost touch; namely, I quit engaging with him for a couple of years due to my shame and selfishness. We reconnected when we found ourselves in Dallas at the same time. It must have been a month or so later when Shelley confronted me and the truth came out.

I met with James and told him my story. My recovery journey began as soon as I saw him come to tears when I recounted my infidelity. Seeing that my choices and behaviors were making a grown man cry helped me realize how badly I had hurt my wife. Anyway, after dumping my reality on him, I asked if he would walk the journey forward with me, helping me to be accountable for my life and meeting with me every week. He said, "I don't know that I can do or say anything to help, but I'll certainly meet with you."

After a couple of meetings, James asked if I was okay with him inviting his friend Kurt to join us. He explained that Kurt was on staff with Campus Crusade at Texas A&M, and he had a knack for walking people through their hurt and was very insightful. I agreed.

After a few months of meetings with James and Kurt, I felt God nudge me to invite a colleague named Kirt to join the group. I didn't know Kirt very well, but I knew I had to ask him. So I went to his office one day, told him my story and about the group, and invited him to come check it out. Reluctantly he did. But he ended up staying.

I met with those guys every week for the better part of two years. In the beginning I talked to at least one of them on the phone three times a day—morning, noon, and night. Later, I still talked to them regularly during the week. Then Shelley and I moved to Denver, and Kurt moved away as well.

Today, almost ten years later, Kirt and James still meet regularly, and every time I'm in Dallas, we get together. I am confident that if my life were to implode again, they would be there for me. Hands down, no questions asked. I am also convinced that, beginning with James, they saved my life. I truly believe that without their investment and willingness to walk the journey with me, I would have ended up alone, wretched, and likely suicidal again. I have a picture of the four of us in my office to remind me that without them I probably wouldn't be alive, much less have a marriage that's being redeemed.

## INSIGHT FROM STEPHEN ARTERBURN

### Willingness

The way your journey to win back your wife's trust will continue to get better is by *willingness*, perhaps the most powerful word in the English language. You may have been reluctantly complying or passively going through the motions of restoring trust up to now. No matter how you got to this point, it is your ongoing willingness that will drive you toward stronger restoration and recovery.

For most of us, every day is an opportunity to overcome the stubborn resistance that has kept us stuck and replace it with an attitude of willingness to do whatever it takes to continue moving forward. All of us are aware of the damage we have done. Most of us desire to make it better and rebuild trust. But the difference comes in the level of willingness we possess each day.

Never allow yourself to "yes but" your way out of doing something that might be the key to unlocking the last sense of mistrust so that lasting trust can continue to grow.

*What and How*

What should accountability look like? How should it work? Do we just get together and talk about the stuff we've done wrong? Is it like a Bible study? How do I know what questions to ask?

These are the kinds of questions I am regularly asked about an accountability group. It seems people don't have a clear picture of what accountability should look like. But the truth is this: accountability is nothing special. It is nothing more than an authentic relationship. It's biblical, but it's not a Bible study. It is about digging into the nitty-gritty of each other's lives and being known. Here are the elements of an effective format for an accountability session:

1. **Opening.** Move from small talk to "big" talk. If small talk is what you do when you are talking about sports, business, and hobbies, then big talk is what you do when you discuss the stuff that matters. It is tempting to let the small talk go on for too long. Why? Because once the superficial, lighthearted small talk ends, it's time to get real, and getting real is uncomfortable and sometimes downright painful. That is why it is important for someone to step up and stop the small talk. You can be the guy who switches gears from small talk to big talk. The typical segue sounds like this: "So how are you doing this week?" "Okay, who wants to go first?" "All right, let's pray and dive in." Resist the temptation to hide behind small talk.

2. **Prayer.** Open with prayer. Invite God into the space and ask him to inform the conversation.

3. **Check-In.** Update the other guys on what is happening in your life and your journey. Some key points may be:
   - *Sexual Integrity.* Have you violated any of your boundaries or acted out in any way? Were there any close calls?

- *Feelings.* What are you feeling right now? This is another chance to connect with your heart.
- *High for the Week.* What was at least one positive experience from the past week? Identify something you are thankful for.
- *Spiritual Journey Update.* Where are you with God? This includes what you are/aren't doing to move forward and what you are learning.
- *Relational Restoration.* How well did you receive your wife's anger this week? What has servant leadership looked like this week? You can also follow through on any disclosure.
- *One Thing.* What one thing are you committed to doing this week to move forward? It could be a particular task or conversation you commit to do or not do.

4. **Closing Prayer.** This is the best way to end. Share requests and lift each other up.

I encourage you to come up with a list of eight to ten things you need to be accountable for and give that list to your accountability partners. Tell them the story around those items so they know how to ask good questions. Let them know what questions you need to be asked as they pertain to these things. What are you likely to want to hide? This is the environment where you get to ask and be asked no-holds-barred, invasive, embarrassing questions. This is where your deepest, darkest thoughts get put on the table for the other guys to see and experience.

When you check in, everyone can follow your list and know what you should be talking about. And remember, it's not the other guys' responsibility to hold you accountable. It is your responsibility to be accountable—to give an account of your life.

## *Where and When*

While it may seem trivial, the place you meet can make a difference. Our group usually met first thing in the morning at a coffee shop, diner, or casual fast-food restaurant like Panera Bread or the Atlanta Bread Company. It worked well to grab a bite in a relaxed atmosphere and start the day on the right foot, but it also presented some challenges. We had a very awkward moment one morning when the noise in the restaurant seemed to hush, and the only audible conversation was ours. We were talking about masturbation, so we switched to a code word: Mickey D's. We would slyly ask, "Did you swing by and grab a Happy Meal this week?" It was somewhat comical, but it allowed us to have the necessary conversation. (I know, you may never look at McDonald's the same again. Sorry.) Perhaps you'll want to meet at your church or at someone's house. Whatever your location, find a way that everyone can make the meeting with as little hassle as possible and commit to it.

Likewise, timing may seem trivial, but it can be important. I really appreciated doing accountability meetings in the morning. It started my day right, and I left the meeting feeling known and accepted, centered and free. Nothing could steal my joy during those days. Sometimes schedules don't allow for a morning meeting, so you may need to pick lunchtime or evening. Again, you should figure out a time that will allow everyone to meet with as few distractions as possible.

You should have meetings every week. Lock it into your calendar and build your schedule around it. You need to know that every Thursday morning, for example, you're going to be at Panera with these guys. Like clockwork. Your wife needs to know the same thing, and she needs to be able to count on it. That Thursday morning will add a Lego each week to the trust sculpture.

In terms of time, I suggest you block out two hours at the table. If all four guys check in and really want to be known, it will take that long. What we found was that almost every week one of us needed the focused attention of the other three. Over time we developed a natural rotation where someone needed and was given most of the time to share, more input from the others, or a greater opportunity to vent. In the beginning, especially, every week seemed to be my week. This was understandable since I was the guy with fresh shrapnel from blowing up my life. But that changed over time and evened out among the four of us.

———◇———

I hope this gives you a picture of effective accountability. The idea is to have a place to share yourself—heart, mind, and soul—with others who are willing to do the same. You are entrusting yourself to them. You are allowing them an opportunity to speak into your life. You're committing to submit yourself to their input and leadership. If it works the way it should, they will know you better than anyone else besides your wife. I speak regularly of the reality that we can never fully accept acceptance until we're fully known, because we'll always wonder, *If you really knew...* These are the guys who will really know you.

One last thing on accountability: whether you believe it or not, through accountability you are establishing a legacy around connection. If you have kids, you need to understand that your legacy of connection is one that will be more caught than taught (although isn't that true of most things with kids?). Your kids will benefit from your connections to your accountability partners, and at some point they will get to see you participating in an environment of mutual respect, challenge, and encouragement.

### Shelley's Thoughts

Our counselor recommended that I approve at least one of Jason's accountability partners. Although in the beginning I couldn't trust Jason, I felt like I could trust one of his friends,

James. So James and I had an agreement that I could call him at any time to check in on Jason.

Jason was aware of this agreement. I think I called only once, but just knowing this was an option gave me a lot of peace of mind early on in our process.

Take Away: Inviting your wife into the accountability process—and by this I mean approving one of your partners and being able to contact him if needed—can help in the trust-building process.

# 12

# The Computer and the Internet

The technology available to us today often creates some major challenges in building trust. If you have anything to hide, you cannot build trust. It's that simple. There must be an absolute open-access policy in your life. That means your wife can at any time and for any reason access anything that would otherwise be considered private. This includes e-mail accounts, bank accounts, cell phones, wallets, safes, computers, iPads, computer files, glove boxes, junk drawers, gym lockers, toiletry bags, offices, storage units, and diaries or journals to name a few.

You name it, she must have access to it.

### Shelley's Thoughts

As we were restoring trust, there were many moments when I realized that Jason was becoming a completely different person.

One of those times was when I wanted to look for something in his wallet. Without hesitation, he told me to go ahead. He had nothing to hide. I couldn't believe it! Really? Who was this man and where had he put my Jason?

So many times before disclosure, I would innocently look for something among Jason's things, and he would become upset. Although I didn't agree with his defensiveness, I chalked it up to his being an only child.

Take Away: Allowing nothing in your life to be private is one small but crucial part in regaining your wife's trust.

For many guys, this feels like a total loss of privacy. News flash: it is! Privacy gets you into trouble and gets your wife's heart stomped on. Besides, why should you care if your wife reviews your text messages, digs through your wallet, or reads your e-mails? If you have nothing to hide, you've got nothing to keep private, right?

I can almost guarantee that any pushback you feel about this emanates from a place of entitlement or fear. What do you have any right to be entitled to? And why? Why do you need privacy? What do you fear will happen if you lose your privacy? Why are you afraid to let your thoughts and actions be revealed in plain sight to your wife? If you want to rebuild trust, you'll need to relinquish your right to privacy. There is simply no other way. Further, it actually helped me become more honest with myself. Living in such a way that anything in my life could be scrutinized deterred me from some old, unhealthy behaviors and also helped me develop some new, healthy ones. It's amazing what accountability and transparency will do!

Remember, secrets equals setbacks.

## INTERNET FILTERING AND MONITORING

One of the quickest and easiest tactics for trust building is installing an Internet filter and monitoring software on your computer and/or smartphone. Internet filtering software allows you to customize the content allowed onto your device. It gives you the ability to block specific sites, categories, keywords, and domains. You can usually set access times and password-protect certain programs.

Internet monitoring software does not block anything; it simply records Internet activity. At specified intervals (for example, every two weeks) the software e-mails a report of your Internet use to your accountability partners. I always recommend that your wife be one of the people who gets that report.

There are a couple of important things to know about these programs though. First, there are always false positives. Something, at some point, will show up on the report that appears shady and maybe even out of bounds. But it doesn't necessarily mean someone accessed that specific content directly. It could've shown up in a pop-up, a banner ad, or an in-page link.

Some of the crazy naming mechanisms webmasters use can also trigger the program to flag a particular site. Anything in a report that looks suspicious should be discussed immediately. It is always telling when a wife confronts a husband about something on the report, and he responds defensively.

*Guilty.*

Second, it is important to understand that an Internet filter is more like a speed bump than a roadblock. A filter will never keep someone from accessing the content they desire to see. Men who struggle with sexual integrity are creative people, not to mention many are in business roles that require them to be Internet savvy. Every filter has a loophole.

If you're a wife wondering what some of those are, feel free to e-mail me. If you're a man with sexual integrity issues wondering what some of those are... Nice try! You can visit my website at www.redemptiveliving.com /resources for more information on Internet filters and monitoring.

## Do Not Erase Any History

If you are in the process of rebuilding trust, anything that can look suspicious *will* look suspicious. Erasing your browsing history falls squarely into this category. Covering your tracks isn't clever; it's childish. I think it is important to be very clear about what this entails. This list is by no means comprehensive, but I think you'll get the idea:

- Internet browsers (Firefox, Safari, Internet Explorer, Chrome, Atomic, Opera)
- Cell phone texts, voice mails
- E-mails (sent, received, deleted, drafts, spam)
- Deleted files (trash can, deleted folders, and so on)
- iTunes purchases or downloads
- Kindle or Nook searches
- Instant messaging services (Yahoo, iMessage, AIM, Skype)
- Internet filters (SafeEyes, Covenant Eyes, X3watch)

Deleting any history signals guilt; there must be something you want to hide. Many guys say, "I'm deleting this stuff so it's not a temptation in the future." That may be true, but if the deletion occurs before your wife has a chance to view the history, it will damage trust. It will only confirm that you're trying to cover your tracks and hide something.

So what should you do about your browsing histories? First, utilize the active truth-telling technique detailed in chapter 8 and systematically walk your spouse through every item of whatever history you are reviewing. Offer to clarify anything that is unclear or sketchy. If it can't be done at the moment, follow up as soon as possible and report back to her. Be prepared to give some context for the activity, the time of day it occurred, the place, the people involved, and any other pertinent details. Then, once you've gone through the list and there is a comfort level with it, you can delete it—with her watching. She may want to take a picture of it to cross-check with the next active truth-telling review, and that's great! That will only serve to bolster your trust-building efforts when the history is double-checked later.

Here's an example of how this can work. With your wife by your side, page through the call history on your cell phone for the day or the week.

Where there is doubt or skepticism about a number, call it and put the call on speaker. Proactively answer any questions and attempt to ease any fear your spouse may have. Once she has seen it, reviewed it, heard the call, and is comfortable with the result, you can delete the record.

## INTENTIONAL TIME

When it comes to trust building, free time can be detrimental. We must begin to use our time intentionally and channel it toward a goal. Many of us view free time as "our" time. It's that time when we don't have a deadline, no honey-dos, no domestic chores—just time to relax and breathe. That time is important, and I think we should all have time like that. But when there's been a gross violation of trust in a relationship, free time is often viewed by a hurting wife as dangerous and risky. She fears that if you aren't busy with work, home, or family, then you might be spending your time acting out again. Violating her heart again, living a double life again.

In light of this risk and danger, you can begin using free time as a space to build trust. Think of it this way: your time is not neutral. Really, it's what we do during our free time that can matter the most in rebuilding trust in our relationship. Consider how you can turn free time into freedom time. In the past, you used free time to act out sexually or maybe to just veg out, watch television, or nap. Now, instead of doing anything negative or even neutral, use that time to reflect on yourself, your life, your relationships, your faith, and your journey. Jot down notes or journal about your thoughts and emotions. Allow yourself to acknowledge the good, the bad, and the ugly of your life. Read books about recovery, marriage, Christian manhood, and your relationship with God. Then journal about your interactions with this material. Record all these great insights on paper.

I'm not suggesting you do a book report, because your time investment is not about the book. It's about how you interact with the material in the book. Once you've recorded your thoughts, allow your wife to read it. Yes, you read that correctly: allow *her* to read it. These journal entries and notes can be a window into your soul that allows her to understand you better and see what is truly going on inside you. Your notes might be hurtful and helpful at the same time, but they will be the truth.

If you look at the bigger picture, you'll quickly realize that her reading about you is only part of the scene, because while you are journaling about yourself, *you're not acting out.* This is how so many wives see it. If you're spending time on honest self-assessment, then you aren't looking at porn, spending time with a mistress, visiting strip clubs or prostitutes, or cruising the Internet for inappropriate material. Your time is being well spent and aimed at the goal of freedom and relational restoration. That's trustworthy!

## DISAPPEAR FROM SOCIAL MEDIA

Facebook, Snapchat, Instagram, Twitter, Myspace, and all other forms of social media can be a double-edged sword. There are many benefits, like staying up to date with someone, keeping track of old and new friends, developing a platform for influencing people's viewpoints, and generally being up to speed on what is happening in the world. Then there is the dark, seedy underbelly of the beast, where social media tools are used for evil: selling and soliciting prostitution, cyberbullying, human trafficking, deception and false pretenses such as aliases and alternate lives, criminal activities including stalking and tracking, and feeding a lust addiction. To that end, social networking sites are increasingly recognized in relational difficulties. For example, a 2010 survey by the American Association of Matrimonial Lawyers (AAML) showed that during the previous five years, 81 percent of the nation's top divorce attorneys have experienced an increase in the number of cases using evidence from social networking websites.

Beyond fostering relational difficulties, these sites and apps are being used in ways that create serious legal issues. Sexting is rampant and in some cases has resulted in lawsuits incriminating those involved. It is entirely too easy to send or receive racy photos, be friended by someone scandalous, or be followed online by allegedly harmless people whose idea of tasteful and appropriate behavior is firmly entrenched in the gutter.

If you are working toward restoration and redemption, obviously social media cannot be a part of your process. I urge you to delete all your social media profiles. As I said earlier, trust is destroyed at our wife's expense, but trust is rebuilt at our expense. Rebuilding trust may cost you your social media presence, but when you think about it, what do you have to lose? Followers? Friends? Influence? Wouldn't you rather gain your wife's trust and respect over followers and friends? Wouldn't you rather have influence in your own home over random people on the Internet?

I regret to say that many husbands push back on this, especially when they didn't use social networking sites in their acting out. But I ask, why risk it? Consider how your wife would feel if you get friended by a former girlfriend or you get a message on LinkedIn from a former female coworker? Why even allow any suspicions? Control what you can control, and be mindful of the things you cannot control and surrender them to God. You can control your social media presence and protect your wife's heart as a result.

I was on Facebook myself, but a few years ago it became obvious that I didn't need to be there any longer. I received a friend request from someone related to an ex-girlfriend. As I saw the request and considered accepting it, I processed what the interaction might be if I were to engage with this person. Knowing they would update me on my former girlfriend's life, I considered how Shelley might feel if she were to view the dialogue. Even though I wouldn't ask for an update, the fact that I was getting one would be hurtful. Shelley would begin to wonder if I wanted an update, if I cared how this woman's life was going, if my curiosity were piqued about what she looks like fifteen years later. No, no, no, and no! But how could she believe my words when my actions (accepting the friend request) communicated otherwise? I decided that even though I had cleaned the skeletons out of my closet, the last thing I needed was a skeleton friending me on Facebook. So I deleted my profile and canceled my account.

I urge you to do this too. Ultimately it is the best thing for your integrity and the safest thing for your wife's heart.

## INSIGHT FROM STEPHEN ARTERBURN

### Sacrifice

There may be many reasons you got hooked on a lust problem. Most of us find that even though we have an addiction, satisfying it gives us a feeling of connection and an instant relief for our pain. Now that you are in recovery and restoration, you are without the go-to quick fix and instant solution to elevate your mood. Additionally, you are going to be challenged to sacrifice what might rightfully have been yours if this particular problem had never developed.

Trust grows when you sacrifice your immediate needs for the greater good of your wife and marriage. When you sacrifice your right to be right so that you can build connection and greater trust with your wife, you will experience much greater fulfillment in your relationship with her and God. Selfishness brings us to a place of desperation. Sacrifice brings us to a place of rich and rewarding fulfillment.

# 13

# The Workplace

For many wives, workplace sexual integrity carries a twofold concern. First and most obvious is your fidelity to your marriage vows and her heart. She is concerned with whether or not you'll continue to hurt her. If your acting out was in any way tied to the workplace, this fear will increase exponentially. If it was pornography on a work computer, she'll wonder what you are doing when you're online at work. This would be a great reason to add an Internet filter to your corporate machine.

I understand for some men this isn't realistic because they work for organizations with huge information technology (IT) departments and a certain amount of bureaucracy. It is also difficult to monitor your Internet usage if you work for a defense contractor. It can be awkward to ask for an exception and even detrimental to submit such a request, giving IT a reason to check your browser history. Some discernment is required in these situations.

If you had an emotional or physical affair with someone at work, your wife's fear of further infidelity is going to be piqued on a number of fronts. Your wife will assume that every woman at the office—not just the person or people you had affairs with—is fair game for you. Why would she think otherwise?

Your wife's second concern about your workplace is her own sense of security. This will be exponentially higher if she is a stay-at-home mom or an empty nester who was a stay-at-home mom or if she chose a career path based on passion not pay. At the moment, she depends on you for financial support.

It's scary for a woman to look at the possibility of being forced back to work (maybe again) because of your unemployability.

I have a client couple now facing this situation. The wife is trying to get a job because her husband has acted out with pornography at work *again*. She feels compelled to find a position and is very resentful about it. She would rather be a secure, stay-at-home mom, perhaps taking on some side work as she feels inclined, raising their daughter and probably having a second child. Instead, she has to figure out how she'll afford life for her and her daughter apart from her husband. She can hardly bear to live with the stress and anxiety of waiting for him to come home saying he was fired. This situation is not unique; it happens all the time, and it only adds to the difficulty of relational restoration and trust building.

Husbands, please understand that your wife's anxiety increases in certain professional scenarios. If you are a teacher, her anxiety will be heightened because it could be extremely difficult for you to secure a new position if you are fired from your teaching position for sexual misconduct. Her fears also will be heightened if you live in a small town where a tarnished reputation can prevent you from getting hired. There's fear if you work in a health-care environment where patient contact can be an issue. The list goes on and on. You must take your wife's sense of security very seriously.

## BOUNDARIES ON THE JOB

Boundaries at work become incredibly important now. If you've had poor boundaries, this is going to feel like an uphill struggle as you implement them. But it is imperative, going forward, that very clear lines be drawn around where, when, and how you interact with women at work. Because the work environment can change our persona, we have to be diligent in preserving our sense of authenticity and self. Your new self must be careful with boundaries, intentional with words, and conscientious about how interactions can affect your wife's heart.

Let's begin with physical touch in the workplace: there can't be any! The only appropriate physical touch is a handshake. If, for some reason, at your work there is a culture of hugs, pats on the back, or shoulder massages, you will need to go against the grain and stop. Your hands do not belong on anyone at work. Nor do theirs on you. If you know a particular female co-worker is a touchy-feely person, keep your distance. Mind you, if that coworker touches your arm while explaining something to you, and your wife asks if you touched another woman today, your response should be yes. To say otherwise would be to lie.

Your wife's question: Was there any physical contact with another woman at work today?

Your answer: Yes, but I did not initiate or reciprocate. She touched my arm while explaining something. So I pulled away and took a step back to be sure it wouldn't happen again.

Believe me, you don't want to have this conversation with your wife. So make it easy on both of you and keep your distance from other people. This goes for personal one-on-one interactions as well as any in the cafeteria or at corporate functions.

With regard to one-on-one interactions with female coworkers, you would do well to eliminate or greatly reduce these. A conversation that requires a closed door should also have an open blind or window. If that's not possible, find a conference room with these options. A closed-door conversation with no visibility is a recipe for disaster and destroys your Lego sculpture of trustworthiness.

Do not have meals alone with a woman from work. Do not stay late to work on a project with another woman alone. Avoid getting in an elevator when it will only be you and another woman. No, I'm not kidding! I once got off an elevator on the wrong floor and waited for the next one because a woman had gotten on with me. I had promised Shelley I wouldn't be alone with another woman in any situation.

If you make sales calls and your clients are women, figure out a way to perform your job without one-on-one interactions that require you to be alone with a woman. If you can't, you might need to find another job.

The same goes for corporate functions. In meetings, it is crucial that you are mindful of where you sit. Sit across from women as much as possible, not next to them. Try not to make eye contact except when talking to them directly, as the meeting demands. Don't have hallway conversations where you'll be directly engaged with women. At bigger events, like annual sales meetings, protect your personal space. Some of these get-togethers are notorious for a raucous time where boundaries easily get crossed. Remember, you cannot afford this. Being a part of it will withdraw all the currency from your trust-building account.

## Minimize Travel

It's a difficult thing to write that you must minimize your business travel. When this subject comes up with a husband who is trying to build trust, he resists almost every time. But I'm a realist, not a kill-joy. Business travel and trust building don't go together.

If you travel professionally, your process of trust building with your wife is exponentially inhibited. It may even be impossible to completely restore trust if you regularly have to travel. Let's address this topic from three angles.

First, for many wives (especially those who have the sole responsibility for children and maintaining the household), your travel is a burden even under the best circumstances. They have to work double duty. If you have small children, your wife has to work overtime to get meals ready, clean up, give baths, follow the bedtime routine, shop for groceries, and more. If you have teenagers, your wife has to work overtime with extracurricular schedules, sleepovers, parties, school, homework, and church activities. The very fact that you're gone, albeit a day trip or a week-long trip, is a burden on the whole family.

If you pile your trust violation on top of all that, it feels like insult added to injury. Not only do you get to mess around and have this selfish double life, but you get to go on trips and enjoy time away from your real responsibilities. That's how your wife often sees it!

Even though business trips usually are packed with busyness and it's not a vacation, that is no consolation to your wife. Traveling for work usually only adds the fuel of animosity to an already raging fire.

Second, travel usually triggers a memory for your wife. This is especially true if you acted out while traveling. Many guys report that they won't act out in their hometown, but when they're out of town, they'll visit strip clubs, call escorts, look at porn, or spend time with a mistress. If that is your story, you need to know that even the thought of your traveling incites deep fear as well as anger in your spouse. If you have to go to a city where you previously had an affair, even the name of that city will draw worry and hatred from your wife.

Anyone who was an accomplice or a co-conspirator is dangerous too. If you went to a strip club with a particular coworker and that coworker is going to be on the next business trip with you, you've already lost trust. Your wife can't trust you or him and especially not the two of you together! Likewise, if you are heading for a guys' trip and one of your buddies is a known womanizer or lacks integrity, you've lost trust by being around him at all. It's assumed that birds of a feather flock together—especially dodo birds.

Third, travel hinders trust building because you are completely unaccountable. Your spouse cannot be sure of who sat beside you on the plane or in a meeting or at a business dinner. She cannot be sure what you did or didn't say to whoever was sitting beside you. She can't be sure that you are where you say you are. She can't be sure you don't have a coworker covering for you and lying on your behalf. Traveling without your wife is not good. It leaves too many gaps where doubt and fear can creep into her mind and damage the work you're doing.

I strongly suggest you not travel. If your job requires it, think about getting a different job. Yes, I mean it.

If you have an annual guys' trip planned, cancel it. While it sounds drastic, I believe wholeheartedly that God will honor your decision to prioritize restoration of your marriage above your career and your own happiness. And I believe your wife will honor that too. If you want to build trust more quickly, be in town and at home every night.

It was nearly two years to the day after my disclosure before I traveled alone again. Now I travel regularly as part of my ministry, and with Shelley's trust restored in me, there is little angst, fear, or insecurity about it in our relationship.

If you decide not traveling isn't feasible for you, here are some guidelines for travel that may help:

- Begin by sitting down with your wife and talking her through the entirety of your trip in advance. Include all the details. Print out an itinerary of events along with who you expect to be in attendance at the events and where they will take place.
- Be clear on your boundaries for conversations at meetings, dinners, and downtimes. Set expectations for what you'll do during your free time (see the previous chapter).
- Commit to texting or calling at regular intervals: when you get to the airport, just before takeoff, upon landing, upon arrival at the client site or hotel. If you are staying overnight somewhere, give details about your hotel and include your room number. Call home from the hotel room telephone so your wife can

confirm your whereabouts, or have her call the hotel room so
you can answer it to confirm.
- Always be reachable by phone (see chapter 18 for more information on this).
- Ask the hotel to block all adult channels to the television in your
room.
- Commit to abstain from alcohol during the trip, especially if it
was a part of your acting-out behavior.

You have to go above and beyond to create as much safety and security
as possible for your wife. Anything less and you're delaying the healing
process.

INSIGHT FROM STEPHEN ARTERBURN

## Be Responsible

Perhaps the most valuable thing you can continue to do, the thing
that is within your power to do, no matter what, is to act responsible
and become a responsible person: continue meeting expectations
and doing what you say you will do. This also means refusing to
blame or shame others.

This position of responsibility gives you and your wife security
that the future is predictable when it comes to integrity and purity.
Your life becomes a beacon for doing the right thing. It is showing
that the tough path is often the right path, and you are looking for
what is right and no longer what is easy or feels good.

Becoming a responsible human being by making responsible
decisions every day and living in responsible ways will strengthen
your bond, restore her trust, and secure your relationship and your
future.

# 14

# Restitution

Many guys report that restitution is vague and hard to figure out in the context of a relationship. My goal is to shed some light on it here as well as give you some practical examples of how to make restitution while rebuilding trust in your relationship.

Let's first define what we mean by restitution. *Black's Law Dictionary* defines it as "the return or restoration of some specific thing to its rightful owner or status." It can also be used to refer to "the disgorging of something which has been taken or to compensation for injury done." The gist of restitution is making the injured party whole.

I believe the defining characteristic of restitution is that it will cost us something to right a wrong we've committed. It's not just about paying back something gained unjustly, but we must lose what's been gained in a tangible way for the other person's sake.

In matters of law, the word *restitution* is associated with contractual agreements where one person benefited from breaking the contract, thus damaging—or at least not benefiting—the other party. A typical remedy is a court order to transfer the benefit to the injured party. That could mean returning profits gained illegally, or it could mean compensating the injured party to make them whole in light of the damage they suffered.

If we apply the legal sense of restitution to our relationship with our wife, it means we have to give back what we took, repay what was gained unjustly, or make up the loss that was incurred. But loss of trust has no monetary equivalent. Therefore, we have to decide what we'll use for repayment.

What profit might we have gained that we could surrender to make our partner whole?

The first thing is freedom. Violating trust through a breakdown of sexual integrity implies that you used your freedom to the detriment of your wife. You've broken the marriage contract that requires both of you to use your freedom for the other's benefit.

In order to make things right and thus restore your wife to her previous state, you'll need to give up your freedom, including your privacy. (We've already discussed this in chapter 8 with regard to open access.) At this point your freedom is not a virtue but a liability, because your misuse of freedom violated your wife's heart.

I urge you to surrender the freedom to come and go as you please, the freedom to have privacy, the freedom to talk to whomever you please, the freedom to be online at any time, the freedom to live without accountability, and the freedom to be lackadaisical in your relationship with your wife and with God.

While one side of the freedom coin is relinquishing your rights, the other side is permitting your wife to have freedom:

- freedom to ask any question at any time and for any reason
- freedom to feel any emotion at any time and for any reason
- freedom to be cynical, skeptical, and incredulous
- freedom to hold on to unforgiveness

Restitution requires you to give your wife permission to be authentic with her feelings rather than fearful of how you might respond, including your defensiveness.

A second way to make restitution to her is to restore respect. Violating your marriage vows by sexual misconduct disrespects your wife. You've injured her by launching an all-out assault on her respectability. Making restitution here means giving back the respect she is due.

Think about the areas of life where your wife warrants your respect. Where can you willfully choose to respect her? Here is a short list: In parenting. In service to God. In service to you. For perseverance in the relationship. In her professional life. In her heart. In her character. In her fears and anxieties. In her insecurities. In her emotions.

An area where I consistently see men disrespect their wife (and I'm guilty of it too) is in dealing with her emotions. Frequently, when a wife expresses fear, anxiety, or concern, I've seen her husband shoot her down by showing disdain for her emotions (justified, real, or perceived) and utterly disrespecting her. Some wives respond with anger and boldness. Others shrink back with quiet reservation. And some seem to be so tired and broken in spirit that they hesitate to express anything else. This is just plain wrong.

We're created in the image of God, and he is emotional. In the Old Testament you'll see a God who feels happy, jealous, angry, and content. In the New Testament we see Jesus, the God-man, displaying similar feelings.

We are entitled to our emotions. They are God-given.

We are designed to feel.

If you want to build trust, you have to pay emotional restitution to your wife. It means not only *allowing* her to feel but *encouraging* her to feel. It means drawing out her emotions rather than hoping they don't get displayed. Ask her to share her anger and disappointment with you. You need to be a willing recipient of her heart and the messy, difficult emotions that come with the pain you've caused.

Another area of restitution is protection. Violating trust means you've violated your wife's sense of security. Thus she feels exposed, vulnerable, fearful, and insecure. And her insecurity is not just concerning you but often includes the world at large.

It is not uncommon for a wife whose trust has been violated to become anxious about many things unrelated to sexual integrity. She might begin to fear for her or her kids' safety, about airplanes crashing, auto accidents, or about your home being broken into.

It's as if insecurity emotionally and relationally breeds a sense of overall insecurity. This is another area where we see how our marriage relationship resembles the relationship God and Jesus have with us. When the protective covering of God seems in question, it's easy for fear and anxiety to haunt us. But under the security of a loving God's outstretched arms, we find solace and a sense of well-being.

For me, when I sense God's protection, I can deal with the chaos of a broken world. Even though everything else is not okay, I know I will be. Here's what the psalmist (many think Moses) said about God's covering:

> You who sit down in the High God's presence,
> > spend the night in Shaddai's shadow,
> Say this: "GOD, you're my refuge.
> > I trust in you and I'm safe!"
> That's right—he rescues you from hidden traps,
> > shields you from deadly hazards.
> His huge outstretched arms protect you—
> > under them you're perfectly safe;
> > his arms fend off all harm. (Psalm 91:1–4, MSG)

When we marry, God passes the baton of protective covering to us to be coproviders with him of security for others. We men are under his umbrella of protection, and our family is under ours.

For a wife, when her husband violates the marriage vows, he destroys her protective covering of security. Thus the effects and vulnerability can be far reaching. To pay restitution means to restore that protective covering.

There is a nuance here worth identifying. For many, the covering of protection over a wife or family is discarded for self-protection. That is the damaging and hurtful violation that adds insult to injury. Have you forfeited protecting your wife in order to preserve your self-image, ego, or pride? Chances are that if you've compromised in the area of sexual integrity, you have.

Looking at porn after a conflict with your wife is a form of self-preservation. Visiting a strip club after a bad day at the office is another type of self-preservation. Using masturbation as a sleep aid is self-preservation.

At an airport recently, I witnessed a husband's self-preservation at the expense of his wife. A family went through the security line and forgot to put a couple of their bags on the conveyor belt. Once they were on the other side of the scanner, a security agent realized the problem with the bags and asked the husband to go back, put the bags on the belt, and pass through the scanner again.

On his way back, the man was obviously embarrassed and exclaimed condescendingly that it wasn't his bag but his wife's bag. He said loudly that she had forgotten it. He threw his wife under the bus to preserve his sense of pride. He didn't want to be criticized for holding up the line by failing to go through the process correctly, so he loudly blamed his wife. You can see how hurtful and embarrassing that was to his wife and how unprotected she probably felt.

To make restitution regarding her protection is to surrender your self-preserving instincts and instead offer your covering at the risk of your own discomfort.

You may be thinking, *Okay, so how do I offer protection to my wife again?* That can take on a myriad of forms depending on your situation. Instead of trying to explain it, I'll give some examples:

- A wife has been hurt by condescending statements or insults from her in-laws. At the next family gathering, the husband is keenly attuned to any such comments. When a hurtful statement is made toward his wife, he points out the hurtful comment, asks for an apology, and puts a boundary in place by saying that his family will leave the gathering if another similar comment is made.

- A husband who has anger issues and is typically rude to people (for example, waitstaff, cab drivers, front-desk people, door-to-door salesmen) embarrasses his wife when he causes a scene. Now, learning to manage his anger issues and to protect her, he is careful about his words, tone, and body language with other people. His intention is to leave interactions with people positive and upbeat, leaving behind the best impression of his family he can.

- A husband leads a family bike ride and usually rides faster than everyone, crossing streets and making turns the others aren't expecting. Now that he wants to demonstrate protection, he rides with them, slowing before street crossings or traffic areas and alerting the family to upcoming route changes.

- A husband, the wage earner in a single-income family, accesses pornography from his work computer where he cannot only lose his job but also his security clearance. Should he be fired, he would not be able to provide for his family and likely would find it difficult to secure a new job at a similar salary. Now that he's focused on protecting his family, he chooses to stop looking at porn, get help, and focus his energy on work while at work, striving for promotions and raises.

- A husband often shirks his agreed-upon responsibility regarding auto maintenance. Instead of taking the cars in for oil changes and repairs, he leaves the burden on his wife, who feels incompetent and inept at communicating with the mechanics. Each time she leaves the repair shop, she feels exploited and overcharged. To protect his wife now, her husband takes on that responsibility and consistently looks after the maintenance of the cars.

There is no script for protecting your wife and family. Each situation is unique. Just know that now you want to find ways to provide a strong covering of safety and security for your wife and family—and then follow through.

## A New Take on Restitution

Now I want to put a slightly different spin on the concept of restitution. To me, there is a more serious aspect that is often overlooked in the definition of the word. If we think of restitution as only making the other party whole, it seems we're only getting back to zero. There is a sense that our work is done once we've given back our unjust profit or replenished what someone lost as a result of our actions.

I think that misses the mark. Our understanding is based firmly in a cultural notion that balance and fairness are of highest value. But we must realize that in Jesus's upside-down economy, fairness wasn't the governing principle he applied to himself or the people he was trying to reach. What if Jesus had said in the Garden of Gethsemane, "Not my will but...wait, *this isn't fair!* I'm outta here. Getting hung on a cross is *not* what I signed up for, God." What Jesus received in terms of crucifixion for our sin was not fair, and there was no balance to be found. His act and the love of the living God were entirely unbalanced and lopsided. We were the sole beneficiaries of the pain, disrespect, and utter embarrassment Jesus endured. He modeled what it means to pay restitution by taking on extreme punishment he did not deserve so that we can receive mercy and grace we do not deserve. He sacrificed not just so that we could avoid eternal pain and punishment but also so we could enjoy life to the full here on earth (see John 10:10). In other words, restitution as Jesus modeled it means doing more than just making the beneficiary whole; it means providing a benefit over and above what the other party already had.

If you've been on a date with your wife and had a bad experience at a restaurant, isn't it nice for them to comp your meal? It is nice, but if we're honest, we probably would've preferred there to be no issue so we could've just enjoyed the meal. Comping the meal merely placates a disappointed patron. After all, the restaurant should do that because it's only fair. Right? But that is a very limited view of restitution. Jesus-style restitution goes above and beyond. The restaurant would not only comp this meal but also offer you a voucher to cover a future dinner for two that includes everything, even the tip. How would you feel if the restaurant did that? You might even joke that you're glad they messed up your order in the first place! Do you see the difference? One makes the person whole while the other makes the person more than whole.

Paying restitution to your wife does not mean you spend the rest of your life in a subordinate position, with no voice or respect and a lack of input. That's punishment, not restitution. The reality is that some wives want to punish their husbands like that. So you may have to endure such treatment for a while. However, if you faithfully pay restitution with your life, your wife will likely move away from punishment and toward forgiveness and peace. Remember, the key to restitution is to make the other person more than whole. I urge you to think of ways to do that in your relationship. Write them down, be accountable, and put them into practice.

## INSIGHT FROM STEPHEN ARTERBURN

### Restitution

Sometimes confession is not enough to relieve us of our guilt and shame and settle the matter in the mind of the offended. Your wife may be struggling to forgive you because, from her perspective, you betrayed her, got caught, went through some kind of treatment, and now wish to reestablish the relationship as if nothing has happened.

You also may feel like you have an obligation to do more than just confess. If that is the case, I hope you will consider taking the bold move of making restitution.

Restitution is a profound biblical principal we see carried out in the life of Zacchaeus. Fortunately for him, all he had to do was make some monetary calculations once he reached a point that resolving his sins—not repaying money—was the priority. If connection and regaining trust are your priorities, it may be more difficult to find what it is you can do to make restitution.

The place to start is to tell your wife that you want to do more than just tell her you're sorry. You want to make up for the pain you have caused. Ask her if she can think of anything that would help you make restitution. If she can't think of something, tell her that if she does come up with an idea in the future, you want to know and will do what you can to comply. In the meantime, you will be working on ways you know to pay back what you have taken from her and the relationship. It is a powerful move that will help her to trust you more. And it will also move you both toward closure on a past you don't want to repeat.

# 15

# No Self-Pity

Y ou've probably picked up by now a theme running through several of the nonnegotiables to trust building: keep your word! The importance of keeping our word has lost traction in modern society. People rarely do business on just a handshake anymore. The deal has to be fraught with contracts full of legal jargon that guarantee a litigious outcome should the contract be broken. The value of our word has depreciated to the point that many of us are cynics.

For example, when a customer service agent tells you that he will take care of your issue or credit your account, do you believe and trust him? Or do you respond with exasperation and mutter to yourself, "Yeah, right." Are you sure to note his name, the time you called, and the details of the conversation? When you hire contractors to work on your house, do you actually believe they'll do the work promised in the time promised and to the level of quality promised? Or do you expect to be disappointed?

Perhaps I'm only projecting my cynical junk onto you. The truth is that I don't always do what I say or say what I mean or mean what I say. Sometimes I don't even do what I mean to do (a function of ADD)! But in my trust-building process with Shelley, I was very careful about setting the mark and hitting it as often as possible.

For most of the wives I counsel, the idea of their husband keeping his word has huge implications. And all of those implications seem to reverberate back to the marriage vows. If you've scarred your relationship with sexual betrayal, then your word doesn't count for much today. And if you can't keep your word regarding little things, how do you expect her to believe you can keep your word with the big things of life, like your marriage vows? It is incredibly important for you as a husband to be intentional about what you commit to and how you communicate that commitment to your wife.

For example, a recent client exclaimed that he should never have told his wife he wanted to go to the gym regularly. The first time he didn't go to work out, she was quick to point out his inconsistency. She snapped at him about how he always says he'll do something but never follows through. Then she pointed out how his failure to keep his word regarding the gym is indicative of his failure to keep his word in their marriage!

If you've been in this process awhile, perhaps you've heard the same thing. Extreme responses reveal your wife's frustration and fear of yet another disappointment.

Another facet of this involves lying. If you've lied and been caught, your word is further devalued. Now, not only does your word lack any worth, your word is known to have been manipulative and used to make your spouse feel stupid. At least that's how it seems to be interpreted. Your wife may think you were insulting her intelligence when you lied or manipulated her.

So how do you begin to redeem the value of your word? There's really a simple answer to this question, namely, by keeping your word.

When you decide to commit to something, even the smallest matter, be sure you keep your commitment. I'm not saying to purposely set the bar low, but I'm suggesting you not set the bar too high. Don't say you'll read your Bible every day when you've hardly cracked it open in the last couple of months. Don't say you'll go to the gym each week if you haven't been since last March, when your new year's resolution wore off. Don't commit to scheduling a date night if you aren't committed to securing childcare. Don't declare that something will change *overnight* when it is virtually impossible to change *anything* (especially character flaws) overnight. The Bible plainly speaks to this:

> And don't say anything you don't mean. This counsel is embedded
> deep in our traditions. You only make things worse when you lay
> down a smoke screen of pious talk, saying, "I'll pray for you," and
> never doing it, or saying, "God be with you," and not meaning it. You
> don't make your words true by embellishing them with religious lace.
> In making your speech sound more religious, it becomes less true. Just
> say "yes" and "no." When you manipulate words to get your own way,
> you go wrong. (Matthew 5:33–37, MSG)

We must learn to let our yes be yes and our no be no. I think one of the most difficult parts of this for me was learning how to handle my emotions when I disappointed Shelley. Sometimes, I needed to say no rather than make a promise I couldn't keep. As much as I wanted to please her and match or exceed her expectations, there were times when I needed to say what I meant and mean what I said.

This came up in some very small ways, such as the time I promised to be home after work. She asked if I would (not could) be home by 5:30, and I struggled inside with saying yes, knowing that rush-hour traffic would make this impossible. Thus I had to learn to say no, deal with my emotions and her disappointment, and then follow through with an arrival time I could actually make. She was rarely frustrated or annoyed that I couldn't make it home at the time she suggested, but she was hurt every time I didn't arrive at the time I committed to be home. The actual time I could arrive wasn't nearly as important as whether I kept my word.

## Integrity at Work

In chapter 4 we noted that the word *integrity* is rooted in the word *integer,* or in other words, *whole.* Further, having integrity means to be the same person in every environment, whether at home, church, or work. Whether alone, with family, or with friends. Whether in town or out of town.

For any man who has struggled with sexual integrity issues, you know the internal anxiety of duplicity—trying to live two lives. We all know about doing one thing but wanting to do something different, all the while sensing our own fraudulence.

I've had moments when, in the midst of acting out, I consciously thought, *This is* not *who I am!* Perhaps you've had such moments too. Our journey toward wholeness and healing is a process of integration where we become the same person in all contexts. One particular context where our train can quickly derail is the workplace.

There is something unique about the workplace. We spend an inordinate number of hours each week at work. We show up to work in clothes much different than what we normally wear around our home. We literally change our external appearance. Already, if we aren't careful, we're being drawn into a different personality. We employ a different vocabulary. Whether in corporate America, small business ownership and entrepreneurship, military service, or blue- or white-collar work, we have a dictionary unique to our professional space.

When I first started at Arthur Andersen, working in telecom consulting, one of the biggest hurdles was memorizing the everyday acronyms used by everyone every day. You couldn't effectively communicate in that environment if you didn't know them. This is not unique to corporate life but rather rife in every line of work there is. So we dress differently and talk differently at the place where we spend the bulk of our waking hours. For your wife, this is a very scary reality. But the good news for rebuilding trust is that your work context presents a fantastic opportunity to add some more Legos to your relationship sculpture.

First and foremost is our *persona*. Think of persona as the personality you project in public. In this case, it's your workplace. The truth is, only you know if you turn on a certain persona in the workplace. Your persona also has multiple forms. Sometimes it is heralded as charisma or charm. It's the thing that helps you succeed or close the deal or win the case or convince an audience. In one sense, this is a God-given gift with profound usefulness. Thus, it would be a tragedy and borderline sin not to use the gifts and charisma you've been given. But these can also be used for evil or, more likely, inauthentic living. The kid who was a class clown is now simply considered funny as an adult. But behind the comedy persona may be an insecure man who uses his gift of quick wit to attract acceptance.

Persona collides with trust building with your wife at the point of interaction between you and your female coworkers. Ultimately, the goal is to simply be yourself in every situation, but when trust has been destroyed between you and your wife, it's prudent for you to be bland, cold, dry, uninterested, and uninteresting around female colleagues. Do you get my drift? You need to run away from words or actions that make you even semi-attractive to another woman.

In *Every Man's Battle,* Stephen Arterburn and Fred Stoeker describe this as being a "dweebman." Perhaps your work persona is that of the man with a sympathetic, listening ear or a complimentary, encouraging Christian nice guy. Or maybe the workplace is where you let loose a little bit and engage in flirtatious joking or conversations with sexual undertones. All of these are hurtful to your wife.

Your wife doesn't want you to be any other woman's listening ear; she wants you to be hers! She doesn't want you to be the Christian nice guy at work and pay Jesus lip service; she wants you to behave like you love Jesus when you're at work just like when you are at home. She's tired of your grumpy attitude and irritability that causes arguments on the way to church, only to slap on a smile to walk through the doors. She definitely doesn't want you to be involved in any conversations with sexual undertones. She herself may not even want to have a sexually nuanced conversation with you!

## Do Not Demand That She See Progress

Men commonly complain that their wife doesn't acknowledge their efforts at trust building and restoration; unfortunately, I was often guilty of this. I hear this grievance almost every week in my office as well as almost every month at an Every Man's Battle Workshop. A husband will describe how much work he has done, how well he has followed his recovery program, and how few mistakes he has made along the way—yet his wife only responds with cynicism and skepticism. In fact, hurt wives are incredibly reticent to acknowledge progress. And wives who are reluctant to trust are usually reluctant to give compliments and positive feedback. Granted, many wives will push past their cynicism to express praise or appreciation for the work they've seen from their husband, but it may be short-lived and fleeting.

In addition, husbands fear that the slightest setback seems to completely erase any forward momentum. The complaining man will usually describe this as "I can do ninety-nine things right, but one wrong thing will erase all of them, and I have to start over." Then they'll add, "When will she start to see that I am changing?"

Sadly, frustrated and disheartened husbands will begin to demand that their wife acknowledge their progress. They'll itemize recent achievements, recount the many hurtful things they have avoided doing, compare and contrast the old and new man, and insist their wife acknowledge their prowess in accomplishing these heroic feats.

Okay…maybe I got carried away there, but that's what I hear from a lot of wives when their husbands demand a progress report. What's the end result? If wives give any credence to their husband's work, they do so with resentment and feelings of being manipulated and even bullied.

So if you want to see your ninety-nine good deeds erased, demand that she acknowledge your progress.

With time and consistent Lego placement, you'll construct a relational framework that is unmistakable, undeniable, and very much appreciated. Don't you agree that it's better if your wife recognizes your progress of her own accord?

This approach reminds me of evangelism. I have never understood nor thought it prudent to do street-corner hellfire-and-damnation preaching. I don't see how that message makes the gospel attractive. Demanding something from someone feels more like manipulation, whereas someone catching a glimpse of Jesus by the change in our life and being compelled to ask about it appears to be a better path. Perhaps it could help you to think about your trust-building journey in this way. The word *evangelize* originates in the Greek word *euaggelizo,* which means "to bring good news or glad tidings." So you are actually bringing to your wife the good news of how God is developing your character as it is exhibited by your changed life—not in how well you can present your case. Remember the earlier section on spiritual fervency in chapter 7?

In honest self-assessment, can you say that your life has changed enough to be noticeable by the world around you? If the answer is no or maybe, you'll need to press in and engage in a deeper way. And leave any self-promotion out of it!

INSIGHT FROM STEPHEN ARTERBURN

## Humility

Another focus for you should be humility. Never brag about how bad you were, how far you've come, or how great you're doing.

Allow your life to speak for itself. Until you regain trust, your wife is watching what you do, not listening to what you say. When you stay humble, God will lift you up. Honor will come, and it will be authentic and real.

You know how disgusting and arrogant it is when others boast about their successes or accomplishments. Don't be guilty of doing the same thing. More effectively than what you say or how you look, an attitude of humility will keep you safe. Arrogance will drag you out of the things you are doing well and convince you they are no longer needed.

*Humility is your strongest link to reality and the honor that comes to those who stay the course.*

# PART 3

# MENDING WOUNDS

# 16

# Making the Past the Past

The past can seem like a constant source of pain and, consequently, a barrier to building trust. But it doesn't have to be that way. In fact, the past can be an opportunity to build trust. Every time the past comes up is a chance to express contrition and humility, to amend the wrong that caused the pain, and to convey your hope for a better future.

I have seen the past become the past instead of the present. That doesn't mean it's ever forgotten or dismissed. But it means that your wife and you can begin to live without the anxiety of worrying about the next trigger. You can begin to relax, knowing that a trigger, while potentially a reminder of past hurt, can also foster intimacy and facilitate healing.

If you're ready to make the past the past rather than the present, the amends matrix discussed in this section will be very useful to you.

No doubt you have seen a scar left from a wound that probably should have been stitched. Maybe you bear one yourself. Maybe it was stitched but really didn't get the healing and care it deserved. The scar is redder than the surrounding skin. It's wider or longer than it should be. It may be raised in one or more places rather than smooth to the surface of the surrounding skin. I have a scar like that.

When I was about eleven years old I rode my bicycle around an oval-shaped track at the front of our property. One section of the track sent me down a short, steep hill that was flanked by a barbed-wire fence. At the bottom of the hill the fence turned and blocked the path, so I had to make a jog around it. I would hit my coaster brakes several feet before the bottom of the hill, skid, turn, and miss the fence.

Round and round, like clockwork, I would go without incident. Until one day I hit a bump in the hill that bounced my feet off the pedals and rendered me brakeless. Frozen with fear, I flew directly into the barbed-wire fence and launched headfirst between two strands of wire. I must have been in the perfect position and on an exact trajectory, because my upper torso went through almost unscathed. I had just one little tear under my arm, but it necessitated only six stitches. My right leg, however, wasn't so lucky. The barbs tore a line down the front of my leg, from about the crease at my hip to the top of my knee, along with another small gash on my shin. After somehow getting home (I still don't know how I got from the fence to my house), I ended up in the emergency room.

My mother recalls that day in vivid detail. Most poignantly, I was screaming in terror and absolutely would not lie still for the doctors to stitch the wounds. Why they didn't just anesthetize me, I don't know. The result was a poorly stitched leg. They closed the wound and stopped the bleeding, but the resulting scar wasn't as clean, smooth, or small as it should have been.

Today, my scar has a different hue than the surrounding skin. It has raised striations through it, and it's about a half-inch wide at its greatest width and about ten inches long. It just didn't heal like it should have.

Amending the past is similar to stitching a wound. It can be clean, smooth, and small, blending into the surrounding skin. Every so often we notice it, remember what caused it, then forget about it again. Or like the stitching on my leg, it can be a bit of an eyesore, consistently reminding us of the healing that could have taken place and should have taken place, but didn't.

When will the past be the past and not the present? I hear that question a lot in my office. People want to know when all this trouble will be water under the bridge. I tell my clients that the past will slowly become the past until the next thing happens to make it the present again. While that may be a slip in sexual integrity, it can also be any number of things that trigger painful memories. And none of this will ever be water under the bridge. It can't. Your sexual failure has changed you—and your wife.

It's like when people say they want things to get back to normal. When someone tells me that, I emphatically answer, "*No!* You don't want things back to normal, because normal is broken! You want a *new* normal."

Part of developing a new normal is amending the past. The past doesn't heal on its own. Memories fade with time, but they don't heal with time alone. The only way to actually heal the wounds of the past is to stitch them.

Let's go back to the surgical metaphor. You have to prepare the operating room, inspect the wound, clean it, stitch it, bandage it, then check it later to be sure it's healing properly. Proper healing of a stitched wound means the opening is closed and there is as little scarring as possible.

When it comes to stitching the wounds caused by infidelity or sexual integrity issues, you must be willing to enter the operating room, lie still, and let the surgery be performed. Here's what that looks like in real-life trust building. Unfortunately, at the time of disclosure, our past becomes our wife's present. That is both a good thing and a terrible thing. It means life will never be the same. It also means life better not be the same. Once the truth is on the table and the mocha hits the fan, amendments will have to be made. The amendments are Legos methodically stacked in the form of a trust-building sculpture.

Now, there are some disclaimers related to this process.

Recently, a wife made a really good point about the amends process. In a counseling session, I was teaching the husband how to walk through the amends matrix and do some healing of past wounds when his wife chimed in: "If this is like step seven or eight in a twelve-step program, then I don't want him to do this. If it's all about him resolving his guilt and getting a pass, giving me some trite apology, then this is a waste of time!"

I couldn't agree more.

If a husband is working on amending the past and his primary goal is remediation of *his* guilt and shame, it'll only hurt the two of them and their journey together. I think it's worth explaining the difference between the amends performed in a steps program and the amends matrix work described in this book.

In a twelve-step program, the amends work primarily to clean up the amender's side of the fence. The idea there, as a part of the spiritual awakening the person has experienced, is that amending past wrongs means acknowledging any pain or damage caused by the person's actions. Then an assessment is made as to whether addressing the issue with the person or entity wronged will cause further hurt or damage. If it appears that bringing it back up will do more harm than good, the amends are made internally within the amender, externally with a sponsor, and/or spiritually with God. Alternatively, if it appears amending will not cause further damage, the amender is responsible for making an apology to the wounded party.

These amends certainly take into account the impact of the wrongdoing on the other people involved, but the impetus for and primary beneficiary of the amends is the wrongdoer. While there can be (and usually is) tremendous power in the process of making amends within a twelve-step program, it doesn't go beyond cleaning up the amender's side of the fence.

Alternatively, with the amends matrix I'm describing here, there is an implicit assumption that performing the amends is going to cause more pain. Specifically, bringing up hurtful things from the past, on purpose, will result in some level of injury. But as we'll describe in the next section, the wounded spouse's pain is usually right below the surface anyway, if not entirely visible on the surface. To address it won't create more or new damage; it will only call attention to what is already there. And the reason for calling attention to it is to promote its healing.

Most wives aren't surprised by something their husband brings up from the past, and when they are surprised, they usually end up thankful that he admitted it. Wives would rather see the sin addressed than glossed over.

Amending the past in our approach is not only about cleaning up the wrongdoer's side of the fence but also requires picking up the trash the wrongdoer tossed into his neighbor's (read: his wife's) yard too! It's one thing to take ownership of the messy, junked-up yard in front of your house. It's a whole different thing to take responsibility for how much of your stuff junked up the whole neighborhood. That can't be ignored.

Wouldn't the neighborly thing to do be to walk next door and ask for permission to clean up your mess? Doesn't it make sense that to expect your neighbor to clean up the mess you made would only exacerbate the animosity between the two of you? For that matter, put yourself on the opposite side of the situation. Your neighbor litters your yard with his stuff, apologizes for it, but expects you to clean it up. How would you feel? Would this endear him to you? Would you be interested in a deeper, more meaningful relationship? I don't think so.

So twelve-step work is about personal accountability and setting past wrongs right. The amends process here is about the past as well as vision casting for the future. While incredibly important and necessary to our individual journey, dealing solely with the past is insufficient for building trust in a relationship damaged by sexual betrayal. A wife needs to see her husband clean up his mess and the mess in her yard (even if that includes some of her junk, by the way), and also make a concerted effort to create a cleaner neighborhood.

Whew, yes, I know this is a tall order. But there has been a serious crime committed!

Next, it is imperative that a person doing amends be in a place to fully own the past and humbly assume the burden of rectifying it. If there is any element of blame or coercion, any hint of entitlement or arrogance, this tool will not work.

Tantamount to humility and ownership is empathy. The crux of this exercise is to empathize with your spouse's pain and experience. If you cannot do that or at least cannot genuinely attempt to, you will only cause more pain. Empathy is the linchpin of the exercise. It's a crucial element in the process of taking a historical hurt that is having an impact on the present and truly making it the past. (We'll talk more about empathy shortly.)

Lastly, if you aren't truly sorry and repentant, please don't do this. Please. I implore you. You'll only be teeing up your wife to get her heart stomped on again. Wives know this. They can smell inauthenticity from a mile away. So if you aren't genuinely repentant and striving to allow God to change your ways, spare her.

Going through the process of making amends with this matrix complicated by any of the aforementioned characteristics will simply create a new item to be amended. You'll try to make amends and wind up creating a new problem to be amended. You'll do more harm than good.

## INSIGHT FROM STEPHEN ARTERBURN

### Freedom in Forgiveness

As the dust settles from your initial efforts at recovery, there is often a residue of bitterness and resentment that needs to be addressed. As long as you hold a grudge or continue to blame someone else for your problem, you are anything but free. When you don't let go, your focus is on a past you cannot change and deeds you cannot undo. Nor can anyone else who might have hurt you. You can spend the rest of your life waiting for them to come to you and accept responsibility for their part in whatever happened. If you let that happen, your life is on lockdown and that other person holds the key. But when you do what Christ did and forgive even the unforgiveable, you set yourself free. You don't do anything for the person who hurt you. They still have to deal with the consequences and shame of their own behavior.

As long as you focus on issues big and small in the past, you remain back there with them—back where all the sin and indiscretion happened. The only way to move forward with freedom is to forgive. Not necessarily because someone deserves it, but because you deserve to be free, and you cannot be free unless you release the past by forgiving others and yourself. If you are full of resentment, anger, and bitterness, you're feeling the symptoms of a lack of forgiveness. Do the work of grieving and understanding so you can forgive and be free.

It is always easier to forgive someone when you have accepted responsibility for your own behavior and opened up about it. And it's not just easier to forgive, but it's also the beginning of your own soul's healing.

# 17

# The Amends Matrix

B efore looking at the matrix itself, let me set up how you should use it. It's very important that you clearly explain to your wife what you mean when you are making amends. As a man in the middle of this journey, you often cannot prove what you aren't doing wrong. You can only prove what you are doing right, and the amends matrix tool can help show what you're doing right.

Like several of the tools outlined in this book, the amends matrix will help your wife see that your behavior has changed for the better. This is critical in trust building. She doesn't want to try to trust the same old guy, because she knows where that gets her: hurt and disappointed. She wants to trust a new man, which may or may not be you, depending on how you allow God to work in your heart and life.

So it's critically important to tell her that you are making amends. This is how I said it to my wife: "Shelley, I want to make amends with you regarding the past. Can I do that with you now?"

This lets your wife know that you are deliberately carving out time and space for this very specific relational interaction. You don't want to make amends in the middle of a passing conversation about inconsequential, superfluous things. Amends must be done at a unique time and in a specific space so your wife will notice and remember.

Too many times I hear a wife in my office bring something up from the past, and her husband—defensive and/or defeated—insists that he's already made amends for it. They'll banter for a minute about it, and inevitably he'll say he made amends in the middle of a conversation about such and such, and she'll say she didn't catch it.

*Ugh.* What a wasted opportunity!

Please take my advice and save both of you the headache. If you're going to use this tool to make amends, frame it right and make it count.

If you initiate the amends, and your wife declines to hear it, you aren't off the hook. She'll remember and you should too. Make sure you bring it back up before she does. In fact, I strongly encourage you to bring it back up before both of you go to sleep that night. If it's bedtime when you bring it up and she declines, pick it back up first thing in the morning.

You build trust when you are the initiator and re-initiator of things like this. You lose trust, or at the very least forfeit an opportunity to build trust, when you forget about it or intentionally leave it hanging.

Also, I urge you to make a copy of the amends matrix template (see page 199), fill in the boxes, and bring it with you to do the amends. Read from the page if you need to. I have yet to hear a wife say that reading demeans, devalues, or in any way belittles the amends. In fact, I've had more than one wife say she thinks it's cute when her husband whips out his handy amends matrix, because she knows there's about to be a meaningful conversation.

## THE AMENDS MATRIX

The seven steps of the amends matrix , found on page 199, are outlined here. As you move through the matrix, you are taking your spouse on a journey from today to the past and into the future.

I suggest you set aside some time to write out your amends before actually making/communicating them. Use the time to authentically connect to each step and write out the key points of what you want to say. In the middle of communicating with your wife (which feels very stressful for many men), it can be difficult to find the right words to say. When you plan your amends and work through it ahead of time on your own, you won't have that kind of pressure. Now let's start with the first step.

## Step 1: Trace the Touch Point

Identify what event is taking place in the present that has a touch point in the past. You're looking for experiences that can be connected to painful emotions for your wife such as shame, disappointment, mistrust, or fear. These events may be connected to sexual integrity issues, but they could be separate and distinct, indicative of your hurtful character traits. When you notice the connection, it's important to ask yourself what and how it is connected. Men usually experience this as guilt and shame, but it can also be noticed as anger. A touch point is occurring when you get a sense that the current situation or circumstance is familiar in a negative way.

Let me be absolutely clear: you're looking for things that might trigger your wife's pain. When you identify something, you should attempt to connect with why it would trigger her pain. Once you connect with it, you are ready to move to step two.

When you perform the amends, you should begin by clearly stating what you realize in the present is connected to the past. Your job is to describe the current situation you've identified. For example:

- Sitting in a restaurant together. In the past your attention would have been everywhere but on your wife.
- Talking to women at an event or gathering. In the past you would have ogled them as objects, not people, so that you could not maintain eye contact but instead focused on their anatomy.
- Sitting at a title company, closing on a house. You once had an affair with a woman who worked at a title company.
- Buying your wife flowers out of sincere love for her. In the past you purchased flowers out of guilt over your secret behaviors.

- Saving money for an adoption. You once delayed the adoption process due to your spending money at strip clubs.
- Driving by a particular restaurant, hotel, club, park, or other place. Any of these was near where you met your mistress.
- Coming home from work angry and stressed out. In the past you would always take out your frustration on your family.

### Step 2: Tap into the Past

As difficult as it is, this is where you begin to describe what you've done to cause harm in the relationship and break trust. This is the past. I know it feels incredibly counterintuitive to bring this up. Almost the last thing you want to do is rehash what you've done, as if she—and you—need a reminder. Men often push back here, claiming that digging up the past will only make their wife more angry and resentful and will delay healing.

I disagree, and I have experience. First, you must understand that digging up the past is a misconception. It isn't buried; it's already up. So you aren't digging up anything; you're simply calling attention to what is already present and visible. It's one of many elephants squeezed into the room.

So many times when a wife talks about the past and is very hurt and angry, half the emotion is a result of *her* having to bring it up. You can save her this heartache. Allowing her to be angry and resentful is part of her healing.

Second, if the pain and anger don't come out now, in a healthy way, they will ooze out later in unhealthy ways. It is so sad to see one spouse's contempt for the other bleeding out in snippy comments, condemning looks, and hostile body language. If you want to get beyond this someday, today is the day to start. Bring it up.

Bringing up the past for healing is different than digging up the past for pain, especially if you work hard on steps six and seven of the matrix. If your focus is only on the past, without so much as a nod to a different future, then hurt will win the day. If your focus is on a better future while not belittling the past, then hope will take the day.

While a wife wants to forget a lot of what has happened, she certainly doesn't want her husband to forget. She wants you to remember the pain you've caused, hoping it will be a deterrent to engage this behavior again. If you talk through this within the context of the matrix, you're actually reassuring her that you understand the past, you are in touch with the hurt you caused, and you aren't inclined to forget it.

It's important for you to cite specific examples in this step. Sometimes a husband will give this a casual glance and speak only in general terms. Don't make that mistake. Don't shy away from it. Cite specific examples.

Chances are your wife remembers specific instances, and you would do well to recollect them yourself. I'm always amazed by the clarity with which a wife will recall an obscure time when a painful wrong was felt. I've seen women go back twenty-five years to a specific day, time, setting, and circumstance where she felt an arrow pierce her heart, and the wound has never healed. In fact, it never got any medical attention whatsoever. And now, almost three decades later, the bandage gets ripped off and the bleeding starts anew. Back then she needed stitches and received only a Band-Aid. This is your opportunity to facilitate her surgery and recovery.

To perform due diligence on step two, try to replay the whole of your relationship and point out your transgressions along the way. Think through the months or years you dated, your engagement, your honeymoon, and the early years of your marriage. Analyze your life stages together: pre-kids, babies, teenagers, empty nest. Think through moves and job changes. Coming up with specific examples that display your connection to the issue reassures her that you aren't trying to placate her so you can wiggle off the hook of your transgressions. For example:

- On our honeymoon, when we ate at that seafood restaurant on the beach, as well as last year when we ate at a steakhouse for our

anniversary, I wasn't paying attention to you. I was watching
other women at the other tables as well as the female waitstaff.

- I lacked integrity almost every weekend at church. I was gawking
at the women around us and allowing my eyes to wander. I was
looking them up and down instead of in the eyes. I objectified
them instead of seeing them as daughters of God. That was
dishonoring and disrespectful to you.

- Sitting at the title company last week when we closed on the
house probably reminded you of the affair I had with a woman
at a title company.

- In the past I purchased flowers out of guilt, like last April when
I had them delivered to your office. The night before I had been
chatting with a woman on the Internet and went to bed feeling
like the biggest scumbag.

- I spent our money, the money that should have been spent on
our adoption process, on strippers at strip clubs. Specifically,
I spent eighty dollars the last time I went in August.

- I remember during those early years at the company how I
would bring home my stress and take it out on you, especially
when our first daughter was born and while you were pregnant
with our second.

### Step 3: The Why Behind the What

This step requires you to dig into the underlying reasons for your behavior. It
is too simplistic and shallow (and also not new information) to say you behaved this way because you were selfish or a jerk or prideful. This step is only
meaningful if it includes a description or explanation that delves into the
behind-the-scenes mechanisms that were driving you. You must take sole
responsibility and you must own it completely.

If you begin this step by saying that your wife did something wrong in the past that you were responding to, the amends will only go downhill from there. It will, in fact, be more hurtful to her and something else that must be amended. To be clear, explaining this as cause and effect will be hurtful to your wife.

Further, if you believe that somehow your acting-out behavior is tied to or caused by something your spouse did or does, you should immediately seek the counsel of trusted advisers or a therapist. Your goal here is to explain what you were thinking, feeling, experiencing, perceiving, reacting against or to—without blaming or insinuating causation. It is so easy to justify our behavior as a response to what someone else has done or said. But the truth is, we are responsible for our own attitudes and actions. If we choose to live in response to what other people say and do, we will only ping-pong through life and never fully be ourselves. We'll merely be what someone (or many people) want or don't want us to be.

For many men struggling with sexual integrity issues, rationalizations are a dime a dozen because it's convenient and easy to blame someone else for their problems. This is called an external locus of control. It is the belief that you're not in control of your environment or outcomes but instead are controlled by powerful others. It means that you believe your response to someone or something is beyond you, out of your control. It begins to manifest in an "if she, then I" or "if he, then I" type of statement. A wrongheaded man would say, "If she says this or pushes that button or disrespects me, then I have the right to respond this way."

Such thinking is wrong. It's rooted in an entitlement mentality. Often the right to something doesn't mean it is the best path to take. The right to respond a certain way doesn't mean it's the way you should respond. The apostle Paul said it this way: "'Everything is permissible'—but not everything is beneficial. 'Everything is permissible'—but not everything is constructive" (1 Corinthians 10:23).

Likewise, if Jesus had chosen what he was entitled to and had responded the way he had a right to respond to the injustices he faced, we would be hopelessly condemned to a life apart from God. So when you engage this step, elaborate on the what and the why of your attitudes and actions.

If you don't understand the what and the why, you should seek the help of a counselor who has experience and training in sexual integrity issues. It is imperative that you have a good understanding and insight into this topic. For example:

- In the past I would pay more attention to other women in the restaurant because I was trying to shore up my insecurity. I was trying to make eye contact with a woman who would look back so I could feel significant and desirable. Engaging a false form of intimacy with them meant that I didn't have to risk rejection. I've lived most of our life terribly afraid of your rejection, which is a function of my insecurity, not your judgment.

- I would gawk at these women and objectify them in order to fulfill my selfish desire to feel powerful and in control. They were objects I could look at and do with as I pleased, because I wasn't hurting anyone. At least that's what I told myself. But I was deceiving myself.

- I had an affair with the woman at the title company because I was searching for significance, power, and adequacy. I was desperately trying to soothe the ache in my heart to feel like I mattered. I looked for it in other women because I was too intimacy averse to allow myself to receive it from you and God.

- I had flowers sent to you out of guilt because I wanted to feel some semblance of self-respect and goodness. I saw myself as despicable and unworthy of love. I wasn't sending flowers to make you feel special; I was sending them to make me feel acceptable.

- I spent our money at the strip club because it offered me a sense of power and control. When I had money in my hands, the women were focused on me and my commands. Rather than honor our adoption process, I was self-medicating a deep sense of impotence.
- I would take out my anger and stress about my job on you because I could control you and the kids. It made me feel powerful and in control because I felt so out of control on the job. I considered you an easy target. I didn't have to worry about your response, your quitting like an employee would, your reneging on a business deal. I knew I could take advantage of your commitment and willingness to tolerate my immature behavior.

When you clearly articulate why you behaved as you did, you do two things for your wife. One, you let her off the hook. You provide conclusive evidence that she wasn't the reason for your bad behavior. Two, you provide hope. If you understand why you did what you did, you're less likely to do it again. If you're clueless, you may commit the same ignorant, hurtful mistakes again. If you have insight and awareness, there is hope that you can change.

## Step 4: Presence in Pain

Empathy. That's the entire meaning of this step. In fact, it is the crux of the entire matrix. If you are unable to empathize, this exercise will be meaningless. Let me first explain how I look at empathy.

In general, people explain empathy as trying to see how they would experience a situation that someone else is or was in. They say to themselves, "How would I feel if that happened to me?" But that isn't really empathetic. In fact it is self-centered, which is core to sexual integrity issues anyway. You're still the center of the world if you are asking that question. Can you recall a time when you were talking to someone who was really upset about something, and as they were telling you about it, you thought they overreacted? If you were in their shoes, you would have responded differently. In that case, simply asking how you would feel if it happened to you would result in a completely different emotional event. You might be able to sympathize, but you couldn't empathize.

You can see how this misses the mark for empathy, right?

It's not about how you would experience a situation, because you bring a whole different set of life circumstances to the situation. It is about how someone else experienced the situation.

Another misconception of empathy is that it's based on speculation. The thinking goes that since one has never actually experienced what another is going through, they simply cannot know or relate to the emotional event. As such, they can only speculate and guess how it must have felt to live through the experience.

This also is faulty thinking and sometimes an excuse not to engage empathy. Just because you've never actually been through the same situation doesn't mean you lack the ability to connect with someone's pain who is in that situation. So to speculate or guess is merely a shot in the dark that may or may not hit the mark. It's not empathy.

True empathy, especially with your wife, means getting out of your world and into hers. It means trying to see life through her eyes. It requires taking into account her past and present life experiences, which may both precede and include you.

To engage empathy, you have to extract yourself from the equation and attempt to be enveloped in the circumstance of the person with whom you're trying to empathize. Walk a mile in her shoes. Consider what the other person is bringing to the situation. What has gone on in the other person's life that would play into the hurt you've caused? What is unique about the situation that makes it different to them?

Say you heard about someone's dog getting run over by a car and killed. If you were to empathize, how might the other person feel? You may be able to envision feelings of sadness and loss, but if you found out the person is blind and the dog was a seeing-eye companion, how might that feel? Can you see how the person might be devastated, not just sad and disappointed? I bet you can extrapolate how the loss would impact the blind person's life in a profound way, and there would be a strong emotional response to it.

When you take into account all of the context and what converged on that particular moment in the person's life, you can connect in a deeper way. That's empathy.

Empathy is a critical element in relational dynamics and can make or break a healing and trust-building process. By and large, while you were acting out, empathy was not present in the relationship. If you or I had truly empathized with our wife's pain, we would have been so overwhelmed by her heartbreak that our acting out would have been impossible.

So, with this step, it is critical to take the time to empathize with her. There can be a tremendous amount of healing that happens for a wife who hears her husband attempt to describe her pain without prompting. When she sees that you understand her pain, she no longer has to try to force you to get it.

Many a husband asks me when his wife will stop berating and beating him down by bringing up how much he hurt her. I often reply, "When she believes you actually understand the depth of her pain and can articulate that for her." This step offers you an opportunity to communicate to her that you get it and are committed to not subjecting her to that pain again.

Because this step is so crucial, I urge men to take their time to reflect and engage it. Don't try to wing it. If you try to do this off the cuff and you really have difficulty with empathy, it will be more hurtful than helpful. You run the risk of appearing as self-serving, insincere, and patronizing. If you aren't willing to do the work of digging in and empathizing, don't waste her time on a lame amends. If you dig in, do your best to feel what she feels or has felt, and get it wrong, that's okay. The fact that you tried and were willing to go there will be meaningful in itself.

Sometimes a wife says that even though her husband didn't actually grasp her emotions, she was thankful that he tried. Hence, another Lego is fitted onto the trust sculpture. For example:

- At the restaurant, when I was looking at other women, you must have felt insignificant, undesirable, and rejected. You probably questioned your beauty and your value. It must have felt very lonely even though we were in a crowded place.

- At church, when I was gawking at other women, you probably wondered how I could be such a hypocrite or if I even had a real relationship with God. I imagine you questioned what you were wearing that day and probably even felt anger toward the women I was looking at. You may have felt ashamed to be with a man who would do such a thing. You had to feel alone and isolated. And I may have disrupted your worship and ruined your church experience. Maybe that's why you weren't eager to keep going to church during that time.

- When we were at the title company the other day, I suspect you felt angry, hurt, and disappointed. You felt disappointed that you even had to think about this, disappointed in your choice of a husband, and disappointed that, back when I acted out, I wasn't who I promised you I would be. In fact, I could see you feeling very fearful; if I could do it once, I might do it again. And that was scary to you, I'm sure.

- When I sent you flowers the other day, I'm sure you wondered if I was sincere or if there were strings attached. You were probably skeptical, and for good reason. It might have stirred a deep sadness in you, because so many times you got flowers from me

to lift you up, and then you were knocked down by the revelation of my acting out. I might have made you question my
integrity in the present too.

- When we drove by that strip club, you probably felt inadequate,
enraged, belittled, sick, and discouraged. It may have made you
wonder how I could be so irresponsible and waste our money on
that place rather than taking a step closer to getting our son.
Maybe you even felt hopeless, like I am or was a hopeless case.

- You must have dreaded my coming home. It never seemed like
you were happy to see me, and now I understand why: you were
anticipating the chaos I would bring home from the office. You
must have felt taken advantage of and disrespected. I suppose
you felt worthless too, that I would treat you like a punching
bag. You probably felt scared and powerless when I would yell at
the baby too. Most of all, I suspect you were devastated by my
criticism of your mothering. You had and still have every right to
feel rage and anger that I didn't like myself and how I operated
as a business owner. But rather than deal with that, I shifted my
focus to criticizing your parenting.

## Step 5: Engage Empathy

Here again, we are dealing with empathy. This step is difficult because of a
slight nuance to our tone in expressing empathy. It is empathy versus sympathy versus self-pity. I said previously that empathy means getting out of your
world and into your wife's. It means trying to see life through her lens. It requires taking into account her past and present life experiences, both those
that preceded and now include you.

Sympathy means understanding someone else's pain but not necessarily
experiencing it. We might point out the distinction as being between the
heart and the head.

Empathy is connected to the heart to feel, whereas sympathy is connected to the head to understand. And sympathy may only be activated when we agree with what the other person is sharing.

To sympathize, especially when you disagree or don't see eye to eye, becomes an intellectual exercise at best. You could understand someone else's pain, but that doesn't mean you'll feel their pain. At worst, you might think someone's emotional experience is silly and overly sensitive, rendering you even less likely to be present with them emotionally.

Alternatively, empathy requires that you put aside your disagreement and move out of your head and into your heart. To empathize with your wife means to honor her pain and heartbreak, to vicariously feel those things with her, and to respect her experience, whether or not it's also yours.

The other element of step five that must be addressed is self-pity. Some people take this to a place of pitiful self-flagellation, as if, somehow, self-condemnation will console the other person. Maybe they think, *If I condemn myself, my wife won't have to condemn me.* It's a type of self-protection to prevent rejection and criticism.

Regardless of the reason, such self-pity is not helpful.

The wrong that made this entire matrix necessary was a self-serving act. To now shift the focus of the amends off the person receiving it and onto yourself further insults and injures your wife. I've heard several wives respond to this by stopping the amends process and walking away, frustrated, hurt, and disappointed—in effect, creating a new issue that will require amending. The goal of this portion of the amends is to communicate the impact of the other person's pain on you. How do you feel for them? How do you hurt for them?

Granted, the line between empathy and pity is blurry, but the important thing to remember is your goal: you want your wife to know that you understand her pain and are truly convicted and repentant, fully intent on never inflicting the same kind of pain again.

Also, it is within this step that a formal apology is made. I suspect that if you are amending a past wrong, you may have already apologized. However, an apology in itself does not count as making amends. How many empty apologies have you made to this point?

Far too often, apologies lose their potency because they are not followed by a change of heart or behavior. They are merely words used to quiet a situation or avoid conflict. If your apologies have been empty, now more than ever, you need to key in on steps four and five of the amends matrix. It will bring meaning back to your apologies.

We have an incredible opportunity to facilitate healing in the person we've wronged if we'll earnestly admit it, realize the harmful ripple effect, repent, and confess our ownership. If you do these steps well, your apologies will be credible again. For example:

- What I've done and how I've hurt you, with respect to the restaurant and our time together, makes me feel so remorseful. You shouldn't have had to endure nights like that where I took your vulnerability and your heart for granted and wasted your time.
- To think that you felt isolated, alone, and angry at church makes me feel embarrassed and ashamed. I realize I should've been leading your spiritual walk rather than blocking it. I completely stepped on your heart every time I scanned the other women in the sanctuary, and I'm so sorry. I realize the damage that caused.
- I'm so sorry that being at the title company may have been a trigger for you. In fact, I'm sorry we even have to have this conversation. You shouldn't be subjected to the collateral damage of my sin. I know I was out of bounds and incredibly disrespectful toward you when I did those things. It pains me to think that you'll have to feel that hurt again and go through another round of forgiveness.

- I'm so disappointed in myself for the way I treated you with respect to flowers and gifts. I realize now that I ruined gift giving for at least the near future. I know you'll have a hard time trusting any flowers I send you. I see the hurt in you, and it makes me sick to think that I've caused it.

- Knowing you have to see all these places around town that remind you of the hurt I've caused makes me feel very ashamed. I know I've taken something that you were oblivious to and brought it to your attention in a negative way. You shouldn't have to endure that. You deserve a man and a husband who respects you and our money; not the man I fraudulently sold to you to get married.

- In hindsight, I realize you deserve so much better than how I treated you. You had every right to leave. You still do. I feel disappointed in myself that I treated you that way. I feel ignorant and ashamed that I valued my work more than you. I feel foolish that I let those precious years slip by without being fully present.

Empathy versus sympathy versus self-pity. It's difficult to know the difference and strike a balance. But if you remember that your primary goal is to let her know how you feel for her as a result of hurting her, you'll do fine.

## Step 6: How You Want Her to Feel Now

Now we have an opportunity to begin painting a hopeful picture. This step and the next are woven together around a common theme of vision casting, that is, describing a life beyond the present that is fulfilling, healing, whole, redemptive, and desirable. This step speaks to the heart and in some sense is the antithesis of step four.

The goal is to state the positive emotional experience you want the person to have in situations like the ones you listed in step two. Instead of pain and discouragement, you're trying to convey healing and encouragement.

It again requires empathy, only this time empathy is based on what-if scenarios:

- What if things went really well and there was healing and restoration?
- What if you could erase the past mistakes and create a new landscape for your relationship?
- What if you could rewrite the script to be a positive one, devoid of the hurt you've caused? How would you want your wife to experience you and any situations like the ones you recounted in steps one and two?

This is the essence of this communication. You want her to see that you're taking her feelings into account. The message you're sending is that you've thought through how it must have felt, and through empathy, you can now see what she desired to feel.

Practically speaking, this step can simply be a list of emotion words to describe how your wife desires to feel. But it cannot be a list for the sake of a list. You want to be able to articulate why you came up with these emotion words.

Sometimes a husband will flippantly throw out some feeling-type words. Usually he is unwilling (or in some rare cases) unable to tap into his emotions and dig deep for feelings. He'll look at step four and literally recite what he believes are the opposite feelings. Where he said she felt bad, he'll now say he wants her to feel good. Where he said insignificant, he'll now say significant. Often these words are delivered with a robotic, manufactured tone that at best comes off as insensitive and at worst causes more damage. Simply saying the right words will not go very far. I can tell you that it is utterly unhelpful for you to do this. It usually reeks with insincerity. Your wife will hear placation, like the exercise is meant to get her off your back. If you're only trying to placate and pacify her, spare her the pain and don't try to make amends. If you do this insincerely, you'll only make things worse.

Here are some examples of how it could work well:

- Regarding restaurants and our going out in public, I want you to feel confident, secure, and protected. I want you to see that I am enamored with you. My hope is that you'll feel like we're the only two people in the entire restaurant.

- When we're at church, I want you to feel close to me emotionally and spiritually. I want you to feel trust and security.

- When we're in a situation like that time at the title company, I want you to feel strong, confident, and trusting. I want you to believe that my commitment to you is 100 percent. I hope you'll feel significant and cherished.

- When it comes to gifts, I want you to feel honored, trusting that no strings are attached. I want you to feel significant, special, and treasured.

- I want you to feel protected and secure with our finances. I want you to feel respect for me as a financial leader. I want you to feel authentically loved and cared for.

- When I come home from work, I want you to feel confident and assured that I'm leaving work behind. I want you to feel excitement, relief, and confidence.

Remember, you're looking toward the future. Your marriage may not look this way today, and your wife certainly doesn't feel this way today, but it's what you're shooting for. She may not believe it, may discount it, might even laugh it off and say something hurtful about it. That's all right. She still needs to hear you say it.

## Step 7: Cast the Vision

This step is the definitive vision-casting opportunity. Think for a moment about what vision casting means: painting a picture of what the future will look like. It's the mission to which we pledge our allegiance and commit our investment of energy, money, and time. It's the North Star, the beacon of hope we are aiming for. It's the light at the end of the tunnel—and it's not an oncoming train. Okay, enough already with the lights analogy! Seriously, if we're not running to something, we'll continue to run from something. And when we spend all our time looking backward, we're sure to run into a wall.

Although Steve Jobs, the iconic leader of Apple Inc., died in 2011, even now the bitten-apple logo is probably more ubiquitously associated with the company he led than with Adam and Eve in the garden. He had a vision for what his company could do in the future. In fact, one of the stories after his death revealed that he left plans for four years' worth of future products. He was cultivating a plan for taking his company to new heights and for revolutionizing people's lives with Apple products. He was the kind of leader people wanted to follow. He developed products and services that drew people from all walks of life to be fanatically loyal to Apple.

If you listened to his press conferences or product release talks, you heard him say things like "Picture a day when…" and "Someday we'll…" It's the kind of language that stirs imagination and makes people want to be involved in what the future might bring.

Of course, such talk had to be followed by action and visible results. But think for a moment how many people would have been on board with Apple and Jobs if he hadn't been a visionary? Would Apple have been so popular and wildly successful? Unlikely. Would there be a worldwide response to his death? I don't think so.

Steve Jobs did what visionaries do: They craft and communicate a compelling vision of the future. They paint a picture of a reality that doesn't currently exist, capture people's imagination, and extend an invitation for others to be a part of it, followed by a nudge in that direction.

That is exactly what we have to do with a marriage damaged by sexual integrity issues. A vision needs to be cast for how the relationship will look when there is genuine healing. We have to allow ourselves to dream about that picture. We must detail the path to get there. We've got to create a plan to get there. Then we have to effectively communicate the plan, path, and end goal to our wife. We do that in bite-sized chunks that can be easily digested, and those chunks are carved out each time we walk through the amends matrix with sincerity and authenticity. Then, like Steve Jobs and Apple, we deliver tangible, working examples of our vision playing out in real life.

How all this translates to our process is the way we live our day-to-day lives. As I said earlier, we can't prove what we're not doing wrong; the only thing we can prove is what we are doing right. Our vision, which ideally inspires hope and relational redemption, will become experientially evident to our wife. She will see the change and experience a difference with you in the way you communicate, your body language, your idiosyncrasies, and more. Trust me, she is looking through a magnifying glass to see if anything is different about you. The safety of her heart depends on it.

So take the time in this step to craft a vision in your mind and communicate where you want to go. Express how you want life to be and how the two of you fit into it. Specifically, you want to paint a picture of the scenarios and life context where the positive emotions you listed in step six can become a reality. While your wife may not (and probably won't) completely buy it at first, you're giving her something to hope for. For example:

- When we go out to a restaurant together, I want you to know that my eyes and mind are solely on you. I want our conversation to be rich, deep, and intimate. I can see a day when my level of communication is creative and intimate enough to hold your attention and you'll know my love is reserved only for you. My hope is that you'll feel like we're the only two people in the entire restaurant.

- There will come a time when my spiritual leadership is evident. I will be the motivator to get us to church in the mornings. I'll be the initiator of our Bible studies. And I will be the one to lead us in prayer every night. You will no longer have to kick me beneath the table to pray for our meals. You'll be able to rest, knowing that my relationship with God is stable, passionate, and deepening. I want you to feel proud of my leadership and vulnerable enough to follow me.

- When our relationship is healed, I hope you'll be confident that I am above reproach wherever we may go. Whether to the title company or any other place where we interact with women, I want you to be confident that I am keeping my mind, hands, and heart to myself. I want you to rest, knowing beyond a shadow of a doubt that there is nothing going on behind the scenes.

- I am looking forward to the day when you can trust that any-thing special I do for you is genuine and sincere. There will be freedom for me to express my love and appreciation for you and for you to receive it without an ounce of skepticism. I want our marriage to be filled with special things motivated by love that we do for each other. Further, there will come a time when you can feel confident that there are no strings attached to anything I do or anything I give you.

- I am aiming for a day when our finances are a shared responsi-bility. I want to lead on managing our money while making sure that your opinion, knowledge, and voice are accounted for. One day we'll be able to pay for our adopted child's college education because of our faithful stewardship. You'll be able to believe my spending habits are trustworthy and have your best interests in mind. I want you to feel protected, like I'm not only being responsible for our present but also for our future. I want you to feel authentically loved and cared for. I hope you can one day feel secure about my financial decisions.

- I'm doing everything I can to create a structure in the company that doesn't require all my time and energy. I want to carve out two mornings a week when I stay home until ten o'clock and just hang out with you. Those mornings I can help with breakfast and get the kids off to school. They can be your workout mornings, if you want. While I may have done hurtful things in the past when I was at work, in the future I want you and me to reap the benefits of our hard work by being able to spend more time together.

———◁▷———

This amends matrix exercise can be incredibly helpful for you. It really can heal the past and put it behind you. It is an attempt to connect with past pain and discouragement that can often feel like a hurdle too high to jump.

You may need to amend the same issue several times because it may resurface several times. That's okay, because each time a little more healing takes place. Eventually the past will be the past.

That doesn't mean it will never resurface; it means that when it resurfaces, it won't have the same pain and discouragement associated with it. Ideally, using this matrix will result in healing, a deeper intimacy, and a new and deeper communication surrounding matters of the heart.

# PART 4

# TRUST-BUILDING TACTICS

# 18

# Tips, Tools, and Tactics

These tips, tools, and tactics have helped me build trust back in my relationship with Shelley as well as helped many other couples restore trust. Some guys have a tendency to think of these things as tasks or boxes to check off. Don't use them that way! If you apply these suggestions in that manner, rather than building trust, you may actually diminish trust.

You must remember that you cannot expect your wife to always believe in the sincerity of your efforts. It will at times feel futile, and that's okay. As we discussed, skepticism is normal and should be expected. Your job is to persevere and press on.

There should be a cumulative effect to your efforts, especially when you're using these tactics. Not one of them really stands individually as very important, meaningful, or impactful. But if you put them all together, along with the rest of what we've discussed in this book, there will surely be mileage you can gain toward building trust.

## FIVE-MINUTE RULE

This is very simple: your wife can call you at any time, night or day, and expect you to answer the phone or call her back within five minutes. During those five minutes your wife promises not to assume or presuppose anything about what you're doing. But after five minutes of not hearing from you, she has the right to assume the worst—she is free to believe you're engaging in whatever bad behavior got you into trouble in the first place. Your wife can and probably will feel like there has been another trust violation and thus accuse you of being insensitive to her pain and to the process. And truth be told, she has every right to feel that way. Do not commit to the five-minute rule if you cannot abide by it.

I'll never forget the time when my integrity pertaining to the five-minute rule was challenged. I was working as a regional manager and had a meeting with several people, including my boss and the vice president of our department. I was on the hook to make a substantial presentation in the meeting.

As we entered the boardroom and got situated, I asked for everyone's attention and announced, "I'm waiting on an incredibly important phone call from my wife. If she calls, I apologize, but I'll have to step out and take it."

It was difficult to make that announcement, especially since I wasn't really expecting Shelley to call. I was just hedging my bets in case she did.

Then, not long into the meeting, sure enough her call came through. Everyone in the room looked at me as I checked the caller ID. I met the eyes of my boss, who had a stern and inquisitive look on his face, like he was questioning if I would really interrupt this important meeting for a phone call from Shelley.

You better believe I would! And I did. Being the man God was calling me to be meant answering my wife's call and working to restore trust. No meeting was more important than winning back Shelley's trust.

If you have an occupation that precludes you from abiding by this rule, you must make other arrangements. I've talked to clients who work in an operating room or who fly internationally for major airlines, and they sometimes cannot receive or make calls for several hours. If that's true for you, I urge you to figure out another way to be available.

If you're out of touch and unaccountable for blocks of time longer than about thirty minutes, you have one less opportunity to place any Legos on your trust sculpture. Make arrangements to touch base just prior to being unavailable and immediately following. Explain exactly what is to take place during the time you are unreachable, including the nature of your obligation, who will be present or involved, and the anticipated content of any conversations. Then, when you call after fulfilling your obligation, reiterate exactly what took place according to your setup conversation (revisit the section on travel in chapter 13). Be mindful of how you communicate during those times. Remember, in all likelihood your wife will be listening for keywords, reading your pace and tone, and trying to ferret out any inconsistencies. What you're trying to do is reiterate that you're doing, being, saying, and behaving exactly as you said you would. That builds trust.

There is one caveat to the five-minute rule: technology sometimes fails us. I can 99 percent guarantee you that at some point your spouse will try to reach you and your phone will not ring or you will not get the text. It happened to me one time when I was shopping, and I'll never forget it.

Shelley called and the call didn't show up on my phone. About ten minutes later, after I left the store, a message popped up from her. My heart sank. I'd committed a five-minute rule violation. I had to own it and not excuse it. It is so easy to say, "I'm sorry, I didn't have a signal" or some variation of that. While that sounds like a plausible explanation to most guys, to a hurt wife it sounds like a lie or an excuse. Just own it. I told Shelley I was sorry, I dropped the ball, and I could see how my actions contributed to her lack of trust. I recommitted to the five-minute rule and reassured her that I was not going to stop working at it. Still, a Lego was missed that day.

If technology betrays you on very rare occasions, you'll be okay. But if it happens regularly, you need a new cell phone provider.

## T-30 JOURNAL

One sure way to build trust is to be accountable for all of your time. We've already looked at free time and how to use it in a manner that is helpful. This section is about your time as a whole. In the beginning of my journey to re-build trust, I kept what I call a T-30 journal. You may want to do this as well.

Every thirty minutes I would log where I was and what I was doing. Then at the end of the day, I would go over the journal with Shelley. Sometimes she would quiz me on it, asking my whereabouts at a randomly picked time in the morning.

The point with the journal is not to be able to prove where you were or what you were doing, but to make a good faith effort to be accountable for your time. If you can show, day in and day out, where you are and what you are doing, your wife is more likely to believe you when she asks later. As I mentioned earlier, wives don't want to be private investigators, so a time journal helps to alleviate the need for interrogations about details.

It's worth mentioning that husbands and wives alike ask me, "How can anyone trust what is written in the journal?" Good question. If in the past you've lied about your whereabouts or whom you were with, nothing written in a journal is trustworthy. But that is not the primary reason for keeping the journal. The point is that you want to be accountable for your life, your calendar, and your use of time. Keeping the T-30 journal is another way to increase accountability.

An example journal day can be found on page 201.

I can't count the number of times wives say this is a stupid exercise and that it means nothing, does nothing, and is a waste of time. Then, some weeks or months into the process, they look at the journal. There was a moment, out of the blue, when they decided to see if their husband was actually doing it. Want to guess how it goes when she sees that he hasn't been following through with the journal? Alternatively, can you imagine how it goes when she sees that he *has* been doing it? Many of those wives who called the exercise stupid eventually find a little bit of trust built because they've seen their husband's consistency and follow-through. They end up grateful for it.

## FINANCIAL ACCOUNTABILITY

Another sure way to build trust is to be accountable for your money. I talk about this every month at an Every Man's Battle Workshop, and every month I ask for a show of hands of men who have:

- a bank account their wife doesn't know about
- credit cards their wife doesn't know about
- cash stashed somewhere their wife doesn't know about
- business accounts their wife doesn't know about

Each month multiple hands are raised, and you can see the effects of a lack of integrity touching other parts of their lives. As I stated earlier, a lack of integrity in one area often indicates a lack of integrity in all areas.

Another important reason to be accountable for money is that it's tangible. So much of trust building is about intangibles and things that are vague, ambiguous, and subjective. When there is something unambiguous and objective, like money, you have to capitalize on its trust-building potential.

Again, you can't prove what you aren't doing wrong, but you can certainly prove what you are doing right. There are a couple of ways to go about this. One way is to shift all your spending to a credit card. That's what we did. I still put everything I can on a card, from a pack of gum to a thousand-dollar payment. I still carry very little, if any, cash. As I write this I have a single one-dollar bill in my wallet. So nearly every penny spent can be tracked on the credit card statement. This is very helpful for trust building.

Having everything itemized on a credit card statement also makes it easier to research a discrepancy or transaction that could potentially jeopardize trust. The only qualifier I will put on this method is that if you have difficulty spending on credit and thus amass excessive debt, it may not be so helpful.

I talk with many people who follow Dave Ramsey's method of managing money and employ the cash envelope system. If this works for you, then an alternative way to maintain accountability is needed. Perhaps you can get receipts for all your purchases. Because I am not detail oriented or very responsible, that method would have been a disaster for me. Keeping receipts is tedious, but if you can keep up with hundreds of slips of paper, then be my guest.

Another idea is to take pictures of receipts with your phone and keep them that way. An app called Genius Scan can be helpful for that. Maybe you want the paper receipts and you always have an envelope on hand or you put them in a particular place in your wallet. Here's the thing, though: if even one receipt is missing (especially if it is a large dollar amount), you run the risk of missing a trust-building opportunity. However you do it, diligence is imperative.

If you have a family budget, it's key for you to stick to it. You can build trust by spending only what you've agreed to spend. If you consistently bust the eating-out budget, you aren't following through on what you said you'd do.

If you can't keep your word about a budget item, how can you be trusted to keep your marriage vows?

Sound like a stretch?

It's not.

## TWENTY-FOUR-HOUR DISCLOSURE RULE

Every wife needs to decide if she wants ongoing disclosure of sexual acting out. Some wives simply don't want to know. They would rather live in denial than accept the truth of their husband's struggles. Alternatively, if a wife does want to know, she shouldn't have to play the detective role we mentioned earlier in the book. And she shouldn't have to live with fear and anxiety of finding out. There needs to be a twenty-four-hour disclosure rule.

This means that within twenty-four hours of a slip in sexual integrity, there will be a conversation, initiated by the husband, to share what happened. He should be able to talk about why it happened, what led to it, and the precautions he'll take in the future, and he should reiterate his commitment to the rule.

The twenty-four-hour disclosure rule serves two purposes. First, it lessens a wife's anxiety. Wives consistently lament how difficult it is to wait for the other shoe to drop. Much like the cycle of domestic violence, there is a honeymoon period following disclosure. Then, some number of days after the revelation, anxiety begins to mount. It is subtle at first, barely showing up during any given week. Then it increases in frequency, gravity, and duration. Fear and worry become daily occurrences, and for some wives, their anxieties can hijack days in a row. They live with the worry that today will be the day they will stumble across another porn site, a suspicious phone number, or some other clue that sexual boundaries have been breached. Further, some wives report not only anxiety about the revelation of sexual acting out but also being in the painful position of having to choose to stay in the marriage or not, forgive or try to forget, enable or fracture the family. Understandably, they resent being put in this predicament, and it only serves to increase their anger and extend the length of their healing journey.

If you're walking the path toward sexual integrity, you should consider your commitment to the twenty-four-hour disclosure rule not just as a tool or tip but as a requirement and responsibility. It shows dishonor, disrespect, and arrogance to hold on to this information any longer. It is another form of self-preservation and cowardice. And it promotes insecurity for your wife.

The second function of the twenty-four-hour disclosure rule is to add another layer of accountability. There is, of course, no guarantee that this rule will be respected. But if you will submit yourself to it, there can be an added motivation toward integrity. Knowing you are on the hook to let her know you've violated her heart again can be a good motivator.

And the twenty-four-hour disclosure rule applies to accountability partners too. You need to fess up to them during the same time period. This rule is one of the best things you can do for yourself. I talk with too many men who, once they've acted out and broken sobriety, go on a binge. They soon despair and lose mental clarity. Their assessment of their situation is skewed, and they begin to believe their lies all over again: *You aren't good enough, God has given up on you,* and *You should get it all out of your system since you've already broken sobriety.* What might have been a brief slip with pornography and masturbation can turn into a week-long bender. It might combine daily pornography use, multiple instances of masturbation per day, and sometimes a massage or visit to a strip club. Don't buy the lies! If you slip, practice the twenty-four-hour disclosure rule. The likelihood of bingeing will be drastically reduced. Not only can your accountability partners talk you off the ledge of acting out again, but they can also help dismantle the shame that comes with a break in your sobriety. You don't have to live in a funk hating yourself again. You can experience freedom, perhaps for the first time, from the negative messages that plague you on the heels of willful sin.

## GPS Tracking

To be honest, I'm not a huge fan of this tactic because technology can fail us. Much like the five-minute call rule, there will be times when technology comes up short or malfunctions completely. With GPS tracking, the risk is the same.

Some wives want to be able to pinpoint their husband's whereabouts. This is possible with apps like Find My iPhone. The feature is also available for BlackBerry and Android devices. You simply install the app on the phone and log into a website to view its location via GPS coordinates.

Even as I write this, I'm sitting in my office and testing the service, and this experiment proves the validity of my hesitation. When I zoom in on the map as much as possible, it shows my cell phone to be in the building next door. Now, mind you, this is only about twenty feet off, but I'm not sitting where the application says I am. Granted, it's pretty incredible to get that close, but when it comes to trust building, twenty feet could be the difference between security and subterfuge.

Say you are building trust with your wife and you're eating lunch with a friend. The restaurant happens to be next door to a hotel. Or a strip club. Or a sex shop. Or anything that is a trigger for your wife. She logs onto the website to find your phone and verify your whereabouts, but the location is off by twenty feet. You see where this is going.

If you use this feature as a tool in trust building, you should pair it with other ways of verifying your location. That may be taking a picture of where you are and sending it to your spouse. It may be having your acquaintance for lunch verify your location. You decide. Don't let flawed technology sabotage your efforts to build trust. Again, remember, it needs to be a cumulative effect, not solely reliant on any single tactic.

## WIFECAM

This little trick originated with my own counselor, Bryan Atkinson. At some point, he said, "Jason, operate in a way that if Shelley were watching, she'd be proud." Simple and profound. Hence, "wifecam" was born.

What would I do and how would I operate if Shelley could literally watch a television or computer monitor showing every move I make? She could pan and tilt to see any angle. She could watch in slow motion or fast-forward. She could listen to every word I say. She could even watch a little ticker scroll across the bottom of the screen that details my thoughts. YIKES! Can you imagine? Would that change the way you go about your life? Let me give you a couple of examples where this has made an impact on my life.

- While standing in line at a Starbucks, there are attractive women near me. I might be tempted to do a double take. If Shelley saw me take more than one look at any of those women, though, how would she feel? Yuck.

- As I'm checking into my hotel for an Every Man's Battle Workshop, the female desk clerk is overly nice. If Shelley were watching, what would my posture look like? Would I be standing back from the counter a little or would I be leaning in? What would Shelley hear? Me simply going through the logistics of getting into my room or some friendly small talk and my issuing her a compliment?

- Say I'm in my office, waiting to see a couple for counseling. The wife comes in, but her husband hasn't yet arrived. How do I interact with her? Is it all aboveboard, or is there something that Shelley might hear or see that would hurt her heart?

See how this works? Silly as it may sound, this little trick has helped me tremendously. This is partly due to the fact that I didn't want to lose my wife. I really, really wanted to save my marriage. If I could see life through her eyes, I thought, I'd be less inclined to hurt her. It was and still is a helpful exercise.

This tool also was helpful because it allowed me to have a fresh perspective on myself. When I'm in my head, viewing life through my selfish, myopic eyes, I sometimes miss some of the subtleties of my behavior. This trick helped me to see myself from a different perspective.

It probably goes without saying, but if you're a follower of Jesus, you probably have already extrapolated wifecam to Godcam. The whole thing about someone knowing your thoughts and seeing your actions isn't a fantasy; it's a reality with him. In the beginning of my journey, God's watching my every move meant little to me. I knew God could see my every move, but I was angry that he clearly didn't care about my next bad one. To me this added insult to injury; he knew my next hurtful step and could stop me, but he refused to do it. Thus, he didn't care for either Shelley or me, or he was content to punish me through my consequences, including self-hatred. God-cam wasn't a difference maker.

Today, it's a different story for me. I do try to keep in mind the reality of God's omniscience, and that helps. If we operate in a way that God would be honored by our thoughts, words, and behaviors, we can trust our wives will be honored too!

## WHEN THE TRUST-BUILDING PROCESS GOES SOUTH

This section is the result of input from my clients. Almost every guy I work with hits a point where the whole trust thing goes south. Every word he says is wrong, doing empathy is possible but not probable, and stringing together enough coherent thoughts to communicate something meaningful to a hurt, angry wife seems impossible. Hitting this point usually results in the husband clamming up, shutting down, or lashing out with anger. He doesn't want things to fall apart, but the powerlessness he feels seems overwhelming.

If you get to this place, one of the first things you should do is take a break. A short break—not an overnight kind of thing. It is okay to ask for a few minutes to process what you're experiencing. Sometimes those couple of minutes can be enough to acknowledge shame, set it to the side, engage em-pathy, and thus enable yourself to be fully present in the conversation. If the break you ask for is too long, it will appear manipulative and look like you're pulling the rip cord on the conversation. That won't go well. If you genuinely need to come up for air from the flood of emotions, it is acceptable to ask for a break. But there are good and bad ways to ask for it. Here are some exam-ples (taken verbatim from my office) of the wrong way to ask for a break:

"Would you just relax for a second and give me time to breathe?!"

"Stop talking for a second! I can't get a word in edgewise. I can't answer one question while you're asking another!"

A better way to ask for a break:

"Honey, I want to answer your questions. I want to do empathy really well. Can I just take two minutes to jot down a couple of things so I can focus and breathe?"

"I can feel myself tensing up, feeling angry, wanting to be defensive. I don't want to live this way anymore and you deserve better. I need about five minutes to talk myself off this ledge and come back to our conversation and hear your heart. Can I have five minutes?"

If you take too much time or do not initiate the reengagement, this will not end well. If you ask for a break, and she has to say, "Are we gonna finish our conversation?" she'll only be more hurt. Stalling makes you look irresponsible and careless. It gives the impression that you are ambivalent about the whole process, her emotions, and the pain you've caused.

If breaks don't help, and you're unable to pull out of the tailspin, you might be tempted to think the better option is to simply walk away. Not true. Walking away is as much an affront as blaming and defensiveness. Rather than saying hurtful things or shutting down and walking away, sometimes all you can do is cry and groan.

Seriously. We all have moments when words are inept and nothing in our vocabulary can accurately capture what is happening in our heart. The apostle Paul describes a situation in which words are inadequate: "The Spirit helps us in our weakness. We do not know what we ought to pray for, but the Spirit himself intercedes for us with groans that words cannot express" (Romans 8:26).

Sometimes wordless groans say enough. Perhaps they say even more than articulate, verbose language. Strangely, we know the profundity of groaning amid pain. We have an innate comprehension of what someone is expressing when, at a funeral, a loved one groans through tears.

When I finally started to open up to Shelley, I wanted so desperately to tell her that I understood how badly I had hurt her, but I couldn't. I would freeze up. My shame and the reality of the pain I had caused would paralyze me. As much as I wanted to say the right thing, the words eluded me. Then one evening, as Shelley expressed how badly she was hurting and how infuriated she was at what I had done, I broke. I started to cry, then sob. As I opened my mouth to say something, I had nothing. I tried to force myself to speak, but no sound would come out. Then I started to feel the pain well up inside me, like an elephant sitting on my chest. I could hardly breathe.

The tears kept gushing. I tried to fight them back, fearing she would think this was a pity party or that I was trying to manipulate her. I also feared she would think I was weak. But I couldn't stop crying. A well was tapped that evening that I can't begin to explain. I ended up on the floor in a fetal position, heaving and sobbing. Between my groans I was able to mutter the words, "I'm sorry. I'm so, so sorry."

I have no clue how long it lasted—it felt like forever. I don't know what Shelley was doing while I was weeping on the floor. She was probably freaked out because I was inconsolable.

Unknown to either of us, this, too, was part of our healing. I needed to purge my well of regret and shame. She needed to see deep brokenness and hear groans that expressed pain beyond anything my words could express. I had to revisit that well multiple times too. There were more moments like this to follow, albeit never to that depth again. I learned that sometimes I needed to feel her pain and let myself express it. At times she needed an audible response, and at times she needed a visible one.

## Building Trust with Extended Family

How to build trust with extended family is difficult to address because every family dynamic is unique. I feel a little hesitant to give much input here, but some guidelines may be helpful. Some people come from a strict religious background, and others come from a more "anything-goes" amoral background. It looks different to rebuild trust with your father-in-law who officiated at your wedding versus a dad who didn't even attend the ceremony. Winning back the trust of the family can be a completely different journey, depending on whether or not you committed adultery with someone in the family, for example. (That can be really messy.)

Another factor that plays into the equation is whether or not you've done this before. If on a previous occasion the truth came out, you got help, forgiveness was granted, and the relationship was restored, then everyone sighs in relief and it seems like Care Bears and rainbows fill the sky. When you do it again, however, the family is often hyper-reluctant to go on the roller coaster again. It is going to be extra difficult to rebuild their trust.

Given all the variables, I want to share a couple of assumptions and keep this section short in terms of guidance. First, this section is focused on rebuilding trust with a wife's extended family—your in-laws. I understand sometimes the in-laws are outlaws, but your commitment must remain the same, which leads to my first assumption: *As the husband, you must be 100 percent committed to the process.* I'm assuming you aren't going to shortchange it, that you're in it for the long haul. And it will be a *long* haul.

Second, I'm assuming you have done full disclosure and your wife knows everything. If she is questioned by her family and realizes she doesn't have all the facts, you'll tear down the trust sculpture with both her and her family.

Third, I'm assuming you have or will forgive extended family members for wrongs they may have committed against you. You can't rebuild trust while holding grudges. The bitterness of your heart will overflow from your mouth and in your attitude. Would you trust someone who smiles at you through gritted teeth and whose attitude seems disingenuous? Unlikely. Why would they be any different?

Now, with these assumptions out of the way, I'll offer some guidance on rebuilding trust with extended family. To begin, you need not give them all the gritty details. Family members don't need to know what kind of porn, how many affairs, how many prostitutes, the amount of money spent on indiscretions, and so on. They only need to know generalities about your indiscretions. I believe a wife has a right to decide what she wants her family to know. But my advice to her is to only share generalities. For example:

- There are sexual integrity issues.
- Infidelity has occurred.
- We're dealing with sexual sin in his life and our marriage.

I'll never forget when Shelley and I sat down in her parents' living room and I had to look them in the eye and tell them I had been unfaithful to their daughter. I told them it was more than once and that I had struggled with pornography as well. I told them my failures had been pervasive and had gone on before I met her and throughout our marriage. I told them I'd been a liar from the start.

Frankly, this was the second toughest conversation I've had in my entire life. And I never want to have either one of them again!

Next, if you want to restore trust with your wife's family, you must take *full* responsibility for what has happened. And it wouldn't hurt to take responsibility for things that aren't yours too. Don't make excuses and don't insinuate in any way that your actions were a response to something your wife did or didn't do. Absolutely, under no circumstances, should you indict her character in front of her family, especially her parents. If you somehow

give off a vibe that your sexual integrity issues are a response to some character defect in her, you are by proxy indicting her parents. In effect, you are
saying, "Since you guys dropped the ball while raising her, you've given me
license/reason/probable cause to act out and hurt her." No parent would
graciously receive such a message!

Further, be sure when you're taking full responsibility that you don't
bring in marital issues. Communicate that you are working on fixing you
and the wrongs you've committed in the marriage.

Husbands in my office have recounted how they told their in-laws they
were in counseling to work on marital issues. That's not the truth. Nor is it
appropriate. If I hear a man say this, I suggest he go back to the in-laws and
clarify that he is in counseling to deal with his issues and how his issues
have blown up the marriage (assuming the wife is okay with this level of
detail). Anyone married for long knows both parties cause issues and marital discord, but this is not the situation or time to point out your wife's
contribution.

While on the subject of taking full responsibility, I urge you to communicate your commitment to restoration. In the same conversation about how
you've blown up the marriage, talk about how you're going to put the pieces
back together. Explain your role in that effort, not what you think they need
to do. I was able to tell Shelley's parents that we had a plan and I was committed to working it through counseling, accountability, getting right with
God, and no longer living a double life.

Another aspect of trust building with extended family is to ask for forgiveness and to practice being forgivable. If you are genuinely working on
your healing and recovery, it's appropriate to ask for their forgiveness. You
cannot place a time line on it, though. Saying that one day you hope they can
forgive and trust you again, based on what they will see in your changed
heart and behavior, is a valid part of the conversation. Just like with your wife,
make it as easy as possible for them to forgive you. Work on being humble

rather than haughty around them. They, like your wife, are watching your words, tone, and actions to see if anything is different. Give them something to see and hope in. Live in such a way that in a private conversation between your wife and a family member, she can report that things are different and better. It would be fantastic for your wife to say, "Mom/Dad/Sister, I don't know if it's fake or true, if it will last or be short-lived, but he is very different right now. It is unlike anything I've ever experienced with him."

Lastly, remember that members of her family are on their own journey. If one of them has experienced something similar and there was a marriage casualty, it may be a longer, more arduous process for you to regain their trust. Likewise if they had parents who were involved in sexual sin. Give them grace just as you want grace extended to you. If you walk the walk, they'll likely come around.

I can tell you firsthand that it was a special day, about six years after my total disclosure to Shelley, when my in-laws sat in church while I shared my story from the stage. This was the first time they had heard the story since that painful conversation in their living room. For me, especially, it was a moment of terrifying yet beautiful redemption.

## INSIGHT FROM STEPHEN ARTERBURN

### Serve

Since the beginning of the recovery group movement, service to others has always been part of the healing process. Whether it is coming to a meeting early to make coffee or inconveniently staying behind to talk to someone, all of us have opportunities for service to others. We are to be the hands and feet of Jesus. When you take your eyes off of yourself and focus on the needs of others and then move to meet those needs, you are rewarded with an indescribable satisfaction. And the very area you have struggled with may be the area where you can help someone the most.

God wastes nothing, and all of the pain you have been through is redeemed when you use your experience to bring hope to someone else by meeting a need or helping to heal a wound. Of course, this service needs to start with your wife. You serve her and make her the focus of your deeds, and you will experience the reward of watching her become the person God has intended her to be.

# 19

# A Word to a Wife: When Your Husband Won't Do the Work

L et me begin by saying that I'm sorry. I sincerely apologize on your husband's behalf. I feel personally represented by men who have struggled with sexual integrity and betrayed their wives. We, collectively, owe it to ourselves and the women we've hurt to rise to the challenge of becoming the men God is calling us to be. To bow out of that challenge and walk away from that fight is cowardly and ignoble. It also usurps God's rightful authority over redemption. When we hit the Eject button on the process, we basically tell God that he is incapable of securing our redemption and thus we don't trust him. At the core, we only serve to further entangle ourselves in the barbed wire of our egos. For that, I am sorry.

If your husband is unwilling to do the work of trust building, I can make some suggestions on the path forward. Unfortunately, many wives report that what I'm suggesting feels like more work on their part. Truthfully, it is. What do you have to lose? The day will come when you give an account for your role in the redemption of your marriage. You want to be able to faithfully stand with a clear conscience and assertively declare that you gave it everything you had. You fought tooth and nail, did work you shouldn't have had to do, took on responsibility you'd rather have shirked all in an effort to see redemption play out. So here are some suggestions.

Shift gears to present invitations rather than make demands. Invite him into your process rather than give him ultimatums. When you are tempted to tell him what he should be doing, instead express your heart and extend an invitation. On occasion, your change in approach, especially the language of the heart, can tap into a different part of his brain, where more empathy and emotion are found. The former approach is surrounded by anger, raised voices, and condescending tones. The latter is couched in a calm, soft tone and vulnerability. For example:

> I don't trust you. You're acting guilty. I want to see your phone and your e-mail right now. Hand it over. Open up your e-mail account and log in so I can see it. NOW!

> Honey, I feel scared. Something about the last twenty-four hours has pricked my heart, and I fear that you are about to violate my trust and betray my heart again. Would you be willing to help me feel more secure?

The latter should result in an empathic response, such as, "Absolutely; what do you need?" If not, then you'll have to move toward boundaries.

You need to decide, with the help of your support system, what your boundaries are going to be and what protective measures you'll take if they aren't adhered to. If he's not going to do the work of building trust, meaning he won't be an active truth teller or he refuses to employ the tips and tactics I've outlined earlier, you can choose your own course of action. In effect, if *he* is not willing to protect your heart, then *you* will have to. That might mean you need time without any conversation with him. It could mean an in-house separation. It might mean that you'll need to contact his accountability part-ners, counselor, or your pastor. It could mean you are leaving for a week to stay with a friend/sponsor/family. Or he needs to leave for a week and find somewhere to stay.

Remember, boundaries are about protection, not punishment. The issue is maintaining the security of your heart, not making him feel pain. Sometimes the two overlap. I felt like some of Shelley's boundaries were punishment. I felt embarrassed by some of the folks she wanted to tell about our situation. In the end, she needed to make those decisions for her best interest. Every situation is different, and remember, your course of action will impact you, him, the kids, jobs, finances, and so forth. Don't make knee-jerk reactions. Be thoughtful and consider all your options. Get wise counsel.

Finally, do your own work. In the midst of this painful situation that you were unwillingly thrust into, you can serve yourself by working on you. This might be part of your own journey, where you do some work on things like people pleasing, anger, codependency, boundaries, self-image and self-respect, healing childhood wounds, patience, or even faith.

Shelley says that in the middle of my mess, God became more real and more intimate than ever before in her life. The unfortunate circumstance that you find yourself in could be the crucible from which you emerge more healthy, whole, and holy.

# 20

# It Won't Be This Way Forever!

I hesitate to write this part because so many men say it is deflating, and they feel despair when they hear it. My commitment all along has been to shoot straight and not pull any punches, so why stop now? I think what I'm about to say is hopeful and uplifting. But it depends on the lens you're looking through.

The process of building trust back in your marriage will *never* end. At least, not that I can tell from my vantage point, a little over ten years down the road as I write this. But the process won't always be so incredibly difficult, like when you feel you are constantly behind the eightball. When I say the work never stops, many men envision a future where the same level of pain, distrust, disdain, conflict, and anger is always present. That's just not true.

It won't be this way forever! Continuing the work of trust building will at some point become an investment that yields growth and relational profit, not just payments you are making to service some enormous debt. Remember that God is doing a work in you that he will see to completion (see Philippians 1:6). The journey you're on is changing you from the inside out. Character and integrity are being woven into the fabric of your being. As such, things will get easier. Truth, trust, and redemption will be more natural and will flow out of who you are, rather than having to be an intentional thing that you do. I promise, it will get easier.

We have to remember that it's not our hurting wife's responsibility to trust us again. The burden is on us. We bear the responsibility to rebuild the trust and create a new relational sculpture. And the new one won't look like the old one. It will have some similar elements, but the two will be markedly different. They have to be.

There will be some trial and error. At times it will seem like two steps forward and six steps back. That's okay. It's a process, not a task.

Trust is not reestablished as an outcome; it is a by-product of the process. And for what it's worth, your wife probably doesn't want you to view it as an outcome.

Every wife who sits in my office fears that once trust is reestablished, her husband will stop his diligence and hard work and the relationship will crumble again. Shelley feared this too.

I really can't tell you the date when trust was rebuilt in our relationship. One day, about six years into our process, I was at an Every Man's Battle Workshop in Sacramento and on the phone with Shelley. She asked a simple but profound question: "What city are you in again?"

I began to answer but was struck with surprise. She didn't know where I was. *She doesn't know what city I'm in!* I realized I could be anywhere in the country and she had no clue. My traveling to this workshop did not necessitate her knowing my whereabouts. Quite simply, she trusted me.

I said, "Do you realize you don't know where I am?" We had a short conversation about it and both acknowledged that trust was there, against the odds and against the backdrop of so many gross trust violations in the past. I don't know exactly when the corner was turned and when trust was restored. But there it was!

This may well be your story too. Hang in there. And God bless you.

## Shelley's Thoughts

I'll never forget the first time Jason and I shared our story at a couples' retreat in the spring of 2011. During the Q&A,

a woman asked me how I could possibly ever trust him again. I remember pausing as I considered the best way to describe trust for us. And this is what I said: "Trust is different now. It isn't naive anymore, like trust I would have with someone else who hadn't betrayed me. It's a trust that is earned and real. And because of that, there is a depth that makes it even more special."

Take Away: All is not lost—there is hope!

That doesn't mean there aren't still times today when I need to reassure Shelley of my trustworthiness. Sometimes I still need to work on proving what I'm doing right. Years later there are still times when we have to sit down and talk about trust and my integrity because something she has seen reminds her of how I used to be.

A couple of years ago Shelley was gone for a four-day stretch, and upon her return I wanted her to feel special. So the boys and I did some sidewalk chalk art, put up a welcome-home banner, decorated the table, and bought a cake to celebrate.

She was ecstatic to see all this when she arrived. Later that night, after the boys were in bed, we were hugging in the kitchen, and she abruptly but gently put her hands on my chest and pushed me away. I was a little startled.

She asked me to look in her eyes and then reminded me how in the past I would make her feel special after being gone, but I had done so out of guilt.

She was right. I would act out while she was away, and then, to make myself feel better, I'd do something extra to feel like a decent husband. Her special welcome home wasn't about making her feel special but about mitigating my own guilt.

So this time, she followed the reminder with a simple, direct question: "Is there anything you need to tell me?"

I welcome that question these days. Every time she asks, there is an opportunity to build trust. I looked into her eyes and said, "No." I reassured her that my integrity was intact and her heart was safe.

Back to the hug!

### Shelley's Thoughts

It's true. If I ever have any hint of concern as to Jason's motives or actions, I call him on it. It doesn't happen often, but it gives me peace to know this door is always open. It becomes a small moment in time where Jason and I acknowledge where we have been and where we never want to return.

Take Away: I highly recommend encouraging your wife to ask you if she is ever even slightly uneasy about your behavior.

You can win your wife's trust back.

Not overnight.

But with time invested, employing the tools in this book, it can happen.

The sculpture God is creating in your relationship will be a thing of beauty. It will be something you and your spouse will marvel at, and it can be a beacon of hope to others on their own journey.

I urge you to press into the challenge.

Don't shrink back now.

In this war, there are hills worth dying on. Giving everything you've got to rebuild trust is one of them.

You can do it!

# AFTERWORD

## A Final Word
## from Stephen Arterburn

Do you have more hope for a future where you won't feel like you are always in the doghouse? I hope so. Everything you need to win back the trust of your wife is in these chapters. I encourage you to go back over this material regularly and remind yourself of how important it is and what you need to do.

In every case I have worked with, there is only one reason a husband relapses or fails to gain the trust of his wife: he stops doing the healthy stuff he was doing in the beginning of the recovery and transformation. I hope you won't make that mistake.

In the brief insights I've offered throughout this book are the twelve most important things to work on as you continue to regain your wife's trust. I will summarize them here.

1. Powerlessness will result in strength.
2. Surrender will result in victory.
3. Faith will result in hope.
4. Confession will result in healing.
5. Connection will result in love.
6. Willingness will result in growth.
7. Sacrifice will result in fulfillment.
8. Responsibility will result in security.
9. Restitution will result in closure.
10. Humility will result in honor.
11. Forgiveness will result in freedom.
12. Service will result in reward.

All of these are tremendously powerful tools in regaining and maintaining your wife's trust. Stay the course, my friend. God bless you.

# ACKNOWLEDGMENTS

Thank you doesn't seem adequate to convey my gratitude to the following people.

James Hill, Kirt Ruby, Kurt Hemphill, and Scott Kizer have faithfully ridden the roller coaster of trust building with me. They've been encouragers, motivators, and, frankly, saved my life and marriage.

Bryan Atkinson counseled Shelley and me through the first couple of years. Thank you for not giving up on me even after I gave you plenty of reasons to.

Jason Lohse, without whom this book would never have been written: thank you for the ongoing reminder that God's grace, seen in the redemption of our marriage, shouldn't be kept a secret.

Stephen Arterburn, thank you for believing in me and for your willingness to share what God has done in redeeming our marriage. You've gone above and beyond with your generosity.

# THE AMENDS MATRIX

**1** What's happening now that connects to past pain or disappointment?

**2** What exactly happened in the past?

**3** Why did you behave this way in the past?

**4** How do you think she must have felt?

**5** How does it make you feel, knowing she felt this way? [Apology here.]

**6** How do you want her to feel now?

**7** What do you want the future to be like?

# THE T-30 JOURNAL

| Time | Experience |
|---|---|
| | |
| 1:00P | Lunch at Wendy's: Chili & Dr. Pepper, $3.29 |
| 1:30P | Walking back to office from lunch |
| 2:00P | Client |
| 2:30P | Same client |
| 3:00P | New client |
| 3:30P | Same client |
| 4:00P | New client |
| 4:30P | Same client |
| | |
| 5:00P | Finished work, jumping in the car |
| 5:30P | In traffic, driving home |
| 6:00P | Packing up family, going out to eat |
| 6:30P | Chick-fil-A: 8ct Nuggets, Waffle fry & Lemonade, $7.69 |
| 7:00P | Still at Chick-fil-A |
| 7:30P | Driving home |
| | |
| 8:00P | Getting kids ready for bed |
| 8:30P | Bedtime stories |
| 9:00P | TV - watching news |
| 9:30P | TV - watching news |
| 10:00P | Bathroom, floss & brush, PJ's |
| 10:30P | Hit the sack |
| 11:00P | |
| 11:30P | |

# ABOUT THE AUTHORS

STEPHEN ARTERBURN is the founder and chairman of New Life Ministries and host of the number one, nationally syndicated, Christian counseling talk show *New Life Live.* This program is heard and watched by millions on more than 180 radio stations nationwide, in addition to Sirius XM satellite radio, and now seen on television at www.tv.newlife.com. He is also the founder of the Women of Faith conferences, attended by more than four million people.

Stephen is a nationally known public speaker and has been featured by national media venues such as *Oprah, Inside Edition, Good Morning America, CNN Live, The New York Times, USA Today, US News and World Report, ABC World News Tonight,* as well as by *GQ* and *Rolling Stone.* In August 2000, Steve was inducted into the National Speakers Association Hall of Fame.

He is the best-selling author of several books including *Every Man's Battle, Lose It for Life,* and *Healing Is a Choice.* His books have sold more than seven million copies.

———◇———

After sexual addiction almost took his life and his marriage, JASON MARTINKUS was called to help other men. He earned a bachelor's degree in finance at the University of Oklahoma and worked in the corporate world before being called into ministry. He earned a master's degree in counseling at Denver Seminary, and today he is the president of Redemptive Living, a Denver-based counseling and speaking ministry dedicated to helping men with sexual integrity issues and couples whose marriages have been damaged by sexual betrayal. He regularly speaks at churches and retreats, and he is also a

national speaker for Every Man's Battle Workshops. His story has been high-
lighted in multiple news stories and radio programs, including NBC-LA,
*Rocky Mountain News*, BBC, and the nationally syndicated radio program
*New Life Live*. He, his wife, Shelley, and their three sons live in Denver,
Colorado.

# start a bible study
## and connect with others
# who want to be God's man.

Every Man Bible Studies are designed to help you discover, own,
and build on convictions grounded in God's word.

WATERBROOK PRESS

www.waterbrookmultnomah.com

# every man's battle
## workshops
### from New Life Ministries

the Every Mans Battle workshops are specifically designed to help men struggling with sexual integrity issues. The 3-day experience combines foundational biblical truth with the latest research-based treatment information. The staff, comprised of masters and doctorate level clinicians, have walked the journey and by God's grace have found freedom themselves. They are committed to helping you find freedom too! Whether married or single, layperson or pastor, Christian or not, you will leave the workshop understanding why you struggle the way you do, having a Battle Plan to fight temptation and a group of men to help you stay in the fight!

We've helped over 10,000 men in the war for sexual integrity. Come join the fight!

- Safe, confidential and judgment free
- Held every month around the country
- Aftercare program for sustained victory
- Scholarships available

---

### Some comments from previous workshop attendees:

*"An awesome, life-changing experience. Awesome teaching, teacher, content and program."* —DAVE

*"God has truly worked a great work in me since the EMB workshop. I am fully confident that with God's help, I will be restored in my ministry position. Thank you for your concern. I realize that this is a battle, but I now have the weapons of warfare as mentioned in Ephesians 6:10, and I am using them to gain victory!"* —KEN

*"It's great to have a workshop you can confidently recommend to anyone without hesitation, knowing that it is truly life changing. Your labors are not in vain!"* —DR. BRAD STENBERG, Pasadena, CA

---

**Visit www.everymansbattle.com for more information
or call 1-800-639-5433 to register today!**